SECRETS OF SUPERMOM

SECRETS
OF SUPERMOM

HOW EXTRAORDINARY MOMS SUCCEED AT
WORK AND HOME & HOW YOU CAN TOO!

Hope you love the secrets!
xo, Lori Oberbroeckling

LORI WHITNEY OBERBROECKLING

Secrets of Supermom
© Copyright 2020 Lori Whitney Oberbroeckling

For more information, email hello@secretsofsupermom.com.

ISBN: 978-1-7362836-0-8

SECRETS OF SUPERMOM WORKBOOK

This workbook is best used in conjunction with Secrets of Supermom: How Extraordinary Moms Succeed at Work and Home & How You Can Too!

If you don't have your copy, you are in luck! You can get a downloadable version FREE here:

www.secretsofsupermom.com/SOSworkbook

Print it out and follow along!

DEDICATION:

This book is dedicated to:

The fabulous four that made me a mom:
Kinley, Kaden, Kamryn and Kellen.

All the supermoms out there. May we be them, may we support them, may we raise them, may we know them, may we love them.

TABLE OF CONTENTS

INTRODUCTION:
THE SUPERMOM IS DEAD

supermom (n.)

su·per·mom | \ 'sü-pər-,mäm \

: an exemplary mother

: a woman who performs the traditional duties of housekeeping
and child-rearing while also having a full-time job

—*Merriam-Webster's Dictionary*

"The supermom is dead," they said.

"You don't have to do everything."

"You can have a happy family or a big career; you are going to
need to choose," they said.

"No one does it all anymore."

"But, seriously, how *do* you do it all?" they asked.

Ah-ha! The real question. How do moms who *want* to climb
the career ladder and at the same time *want* to be present
and amazing for their families do it? How do they stay happy,
healthy, and not consistently stressed out to the max? How do
they maintain friendships and relationships? How do they "do

it all" without overwhelm and without guilt? How do they maintain balance?

Hi! I'm Lori, and I am a supermom.

Eleven years ago in the midst of weekly travel and climbing the career ladder fast-track, I became a mom. Fast forward to today, and I am a forty-year-old, married mom of four. I have a successful career in corporate America, a husband who travels weekly, and still have time for family and friends. I have been the President of the Parent Teacher Student Association at our kids' school, run a fulfilling side business as a newborn and family photographer, and volunteer.

"Who are you?" they asked. "How can you possibly do all this and still be happy? How are you not just completely burned out? How do you *always* have so much energy?"

For a long time, I would laugh, maybe even a little embarrassed, and just say, "I don't know," or "I just do it, I guess." I always thought that I was just doing what everyone else was doing.

I come from a long line of working women. My Grandma Marylou worked for sixteen years at Western Electric at a time when most women were stay-at-home moms. My Ahmah Betty—seriously, never call her "Grandma"—was a hospital and traveling nurse for over forty-five years. My mom went to dental hygiene school while pregnant with me and has been a dental hygienist for over forty years.

I remember other moms always being blown away by my mom. They couldn't believe that she worked and kept a spotless house. She did laundry every day. She cooked dinner every night. She always wore makeup (still does) and always looked gorgeous (still does). She took us to soccer practice and dance lessons and school activities. She made quilts and taught us to paint and make earrings. It was like she had unending energy. I really did learn from the best.

I have come to realize that those friends *really* meant the question: What was I doing differently that no one else was doing? How was I calm (mostly), happy (99% of the time), and still slaying the dragons of everyday life? How was I getting so much done on a consistent basis? What in the world was I doing?

I realized that these "tricks" of everyday life I learned along the way didn't just come easily to everyone. Moms were not continuously adding to their arsenal of tools. They were instead adding responsibilities without the tools to handle them—and they were drowning.

Year to year, we seem to encounter pendulum swings. Society fluctuates back and forth. Moms are pressured to do everything and be *everything*. Next, moms should not do everything but should sacrifice. What about those of us that don't want to sacrifice? We don't need to do and be everything, but we do want it all. I want to be an extraordinary, career-driven woman, and I want to be an extraordinary,

I WANT TO BE AN EXTRAORDINARY, CAREER-DRIVEN WOMAN, AND I WANT TO BE AN EXTRAORDINARY, PRESENT MOM.

present mom. To top it off, I want to be the best at both. I have worked hard to gain the skills to be great at my career and the skills to be an amazing mom.

The biggest secret is that perfect balance is a lie. We are all looking for work-life balance. In surveying and interviewing nearly two hundred moms for this book, over 40% said they couldn't seem to figure out balance. Do you know why? It does not exist. You will never be perfectly balanced between work and home and relationships and friends and family and…you name it. What you will learn is how to feel like you are giving your best to your job, your best at home, and your best to everything else. You will learn to take care of yourself. You will learn to put first things first and let go of guilt. This is true balance.

Do you want to be a better mom, better at your career, better at *feeling* balanced, and better at avoiding burnout? I am excited to share this book with you. It includes tangible tools and secrets that I have personally used to make my life at work and at home stronger, better, and more successful. In many cases, the skills that make me great at my job also make me a great mom, and the skills that make me a great mom also make me great at my job. I have backed it up with stories and even with a little bit of research that shows what I have picked up along the way *actually works*.

This book is my way of saving supermom. I see you. You want a career or a business or a side hustle. At the same time, you want to be available, happy, and a role model to your kids. You want to feel like you are serving your family, serving your team, and serving yourself all in the best way you know how. Without guilt. Without apology.

You want it all. You can have it. I can show you how.

All right, supermom, I know your time is limited and precious. I organized this book into chapters that each focus on a secret you can use to become better at your job and at home. In each chapter, I tell you some stories about how the concepts actually work. I tell you about my husband, Jeremy. I tell you about my kids Kinley, Kaden, Kamryn "Kami," and Kellen, ages ten, nine, seven, and four respectively. I talk about work stories, stories with friends, and interviews with lots of supermoms. I tell you about research that proves these concepts are based in reality.

Hopefully, this is a quick and easy read for you that will allow you to apply some stress-free strategies for quick wins. Every chapter even includes just one small step you can take to a better life if you only have one minute to spare.

One. Small. Step.

They say the first step is always the hardest. Let's take that first step together on a path to becoming everything you know you can be, the best in your career and the best mom.

Feel like you don't even have enough time to get through the pages? I am here for you! Flip to the end of each chapter for a one-page chapter wrap up with the key takeaways including those small steps. Call it a supermom shortcut. This doesn't have to be hard! Let's do this!

PART 1

THE KEY SECRETS

CHAPTER 1
SUPERMOMS HAVE SYSTEMS

THE SECRET OF HABITS

"You do not rise to the level of your goals. You fall to the level of your systems."

—James Clear, *Atomic Habits: An Easy & Proven Way to Build Good Habits & Break Bad Ones* [1]

"As people strengthened their willpower muscles in one part of their lives—in the gym, or a money management program—that strength spilled over into what they ate or how hard they worked. Once willpower became stronger, it touched everything."

—Charles Duhigg, *The Power of Habit: Why We Do What We Do in Life and Business* [2]

Every morning and night, I brush my teeth. Every day when I wake up at 4:00 a.m., I make a pot of coffee and drink my first cup black. Every Monday, Wednesday, and Friday, I take a group personal training class at 5:00 a.m. Every day I write in my planner, review my schedule, kiss my husband, hug my kids, take out dinner meat to thaw, feed the dogs, and do so many other things nearly on autopilot. Every. Single. Day.

I have always known the importance of quality habits, even at a subconscious level. I had good habits, but I wasn't intentional about growing them. I did not learn about the real benefit of habits until much later in life as I read books, articles, and research.

One of my absolute favorite books on the topic is *High Performance Habits*[3] by Brendon Burchard. It is a fairly long and data-heavy read, but the concepts are outstanding. In his introduction, he details the things we know about high-performing humans that are unlike others. As I re-read this book for the third time, I thought how you could replace the words "high performers" with "supermoms" in every case and be defining a supermom. Here are some of the things he says about "high performers" with those words replaced with the word "supermoms":

- Supermoms are more successful than their peers, yet they are less stressed.
- Supermoms love challenges and are more confident that they will achieve their goals despite adversity.
- Supermoms are healthier than their peers.
- Supermoms are happy.
- Supermoms are admired.
- Supermoms get better grades and reach higher positions of success.

- Supermoms work passionately regardless of traditional rewards.
- Supermoms are assertive (for the right reasons).
- Supermoms see and serve beyond their strengths.
- Supermoms are uniquely productive—they've mastered prolific quality output.
- Supermoms are adaptive servant leaders.

Why can these high-performing moms keep all the plates of life spinning? How do they keep a successful career and a happy home not to mention friends and hobbies and everything else? Habits.

Supermoms have developed routines, whether intentionally or not, that set them up to succeed every day. These systems become habits, they are nearly automatic, and they perpetuate success.

Imagine if you had to think hard to brush your teeth or tie your shoes. Your brainpower would be wasted on minutia, and nothing would be left for more challenging endeavors. Now think about how easy things would be if other tasks of your day were just as easy as brushing your teeth.

Habits have been widely studied and are found to be responsible for 60% of your daily activities and as much as 40% of our experience of the positive and negative of our day. These percentages are huge. When you have habits that set you up for positive outcomes, you can change your life.

I am starting this book with a discussion of habits because so many of the secrets in this book require strong habits and systems to develop the skill. If you don't have good habits, or an understanding of how to change your habits, you can't gain the skill you need to be the happiest and most fulfilled.

———————————

What habits are critical to the success of supermoms? I interviewed and surveyed nearly two hundred moms when creating this book and asked them, "What is your number one strategy for keeping it together as a mom?" Essentially, what are your habits that allow you to be successful?

The number one response was keeping a planner, calendar, or lists of to-dos. Staying organized is the best way high-performing moms keep things together. We talk more about time management and managing calendars and lists in Chapter 13.

The next most common response that allowed moms to maintain energy and "keep it together" was self-care. Supermoms know that giving themselves a chance to rest, to restore energy, and to have fun are critically important to keep going. Head to Chapter 10 for more information on rest and some quick but effective strategies you can do in just five minutes.

Finally, having a positive mindset, keeping things in perspective, and looking at the big picture help these moms de-stress and allow them to be great moms in the midst of busy lives. We dive deeper into mindset in Chapter 11.

These supermoms also mentioned asking for help, exercise, prayer, coffee, books, sleep, music and a solid morning routine as habits that help them every day. We touch on so many of these right in the pages of this book.

This is all well and good, but how do we actually create good habits? How do we change bad habits so we can be more successful at work and home?

STOP CHANGING PROCESSES

Imagine yourself getting into your car every morning. You buckle your seatbelt, put on your favorite radio station, and put the car in gear. Now, imagine that you take a completely different way to work every day. Each day, you take different roads. Sometimes you use the freeway. Sometimes you take side streets. Sometimes you take a back alley. Would this be efficient? Of course not.

First of all, some routes would definitely take you much longer than others. The biggest drawback is that each day you would have to really focus on your route. You would need to put all your mental energy into making sure you took the right roads to get to your destination.

Instead, what do you do? You take the same exact streets every day. Do you think about this every day? Likely not. You might even get to work some days and not clearly remember the whole drive. You can do this because it has become a habit. The habit is so ingrained that it can allow you to focus on other things while driving like listening to a podcast or an audiobook.

The most important benefit of systems, routines, or *habits* is that you can spend less energy on the unimportant and more mental energy on the big goals. When you continually change processes, you prevent habit formation and force yourself to think harder about your tasks. You must put systems in place that allow you to put some activities on autopilot. The tasks get done, but not with loads of effort.

Think about your morning. We dive deeper into morning routines in Chapter 3, but think about your morning as it is right now. Is it different every day? Are you constantly changing the order and the flow of what has to happen? Sometimes you shower. Sometimes you look at your planner. Sometimes you make the kids' lunches. Does it feel chaotic? I have a feeling it might.

What if your daily schedule changes? The system doesn't have to be the exact same every day, but there should be a consistent flow to your days and week as a whole. I have a friend who is an ICU nurse. Some days she is home with her kids, and some days she is working twelve-hour shifts. Every day does not look the same, but the days she is home have the same morning routine. The days she works have the same morning routine. Even though every single day does not look the same, the flow from week to week has a system.

> **THE MOST IMPORTANT BENEFIT OF SYSTEMS, ROUTINES, OR HABITS IS THAT YOU CAN SPEND LESS ENERGY ON THE UNIMPORTANT AND MORE MENTAL ENERGY ON THE BIG GOALS.**

On a piece of paper or in your Secrets of Supermom Workbook, brainstorm parts of your day that could have a more stable, consistent routine. Where could your put your own or your family's habits into a system? How can you make your day easier?

(FORGOT TO DOWNLOAD YOUR SECRETS OF SUPERMOM WORKBOOK?
YOU CAN GET YOUR COPY AT
WWW.SECRETSOFSUPERMOM.COM/SOSWORKBOOK.)

EVALUATE YOUR HABIT LOOPS

The basics of habit research show that habits form when you have a cue, a response and a reward. For example, every time you hear the dog scratch at the door (the cue), you get up and let her outside (the response), and she doesn't pee on your rug (the reward). Every time you drive home from your parent's house you pass by a Dairy Queen (the cue), you pop in the drive-thru (the response), and get a delicious ice cream cone (the reward).

Charles Duhigg, the author of *The Power of Habit*, says that you "can't extinguish a bad habit, you can only change it."[4] He means that simply getting rid of habits, especially deeply ingrained habits, is nearly impossible. Instead, you can evaluate the cue, the response or routine, and the reward. Once you know the feelings and reactions behind the action, you can invoke change.

Perhaps you have developed an unwelcome habit of drinking two glasses of wine every night. I am not talking about alcohol abuse, which is outside the scope of this book, but an alcohol habit that you would like to change. Maybe it is affecting your sleep or making you groggy in the morning.

You could simply say, "I am not drinking wine at night anymore." You could rely on simple willpower. Statistically speaking, you are unlikely to be successful with the change long term.

Instead, you need to evaluate the cue and the routine that brings the reward—the relaxation from the wine. After evaluating each piece of the habit loop, you can find an effective way to change the habit.

- Cue: You close your laptop in your home office indicating the end of your workday.
- Routine: You walk out of your office into the kitchen to start dinner, pour a glass of wine, and take a sip.
- Reward: You feel relaxed.

It would be fairly difficult to change the cue. Your workday will have to end.

Let's look at the routine and the reward. How are you feeling as you walk into the kitchen? Are you rushed? Are you stressed? Are you dreading the dinner prep? Did you just come out of a super stressful day at work?

You might realize that your actual goal is to feel relaxed. You want this reward and don't want that to change. Now you know that in order to change the wine habit, you need to change the routine.

What other things help you to feel relaxed in other situations? Is it talking with your best friend, taking a walk, doing a quick meditation, or perhaps reading a book?

When thinking about how to change the routine, make sure not to replace the unwanted habit with another unwanted habit. For example, if eating chocolate also makes you feel relaxed, you might be tempted to replace the wine with chocolate. If you don't want to be eating chocolate every night either, don't let that be the replacement routine.

Let's say you have decided that taking a quick walk or reading a book would also help you feel relaxed. Here is where you change the routine. Every day, after you close your laptop, you head out the door for a brisk walk with your newest audiobook instead of straight into the kitchen. You immediately feel relaxed.

Keeping the cue and the reward allows you to get the same emotional response from a better routine. By evaluating the habit loop, you can make positive changes when habits are not serving you.

FOLLOW JAMES CLEAR'S FOUR LAWS

James Clear, author of *Atomic Habits: Tiny Changes, Remarkable Results*,[5] says there are four laws to habit change:

- Make It Obvious
- Make it Attractive
- Make it Easy
- Make it Satisfying

Sounds easy enough, right? He also says to break a bad habit you can use the reverse of these laws:

- Make it Invisible
- Make it Unattractive
- Make it Difficult
- Make it Unsatisfying

Let me share a few examples of how these concepts work from my life.

Last year, I bought this face oil that is supposed to go on your face every night to reduce wrinkles. I liked the idea of reducing wrinkles, but I found that I only remembered to put it on about two nights per week despite truly wanting the benefit of the oil. I decided that I would move the small bottle to my nightstand instead of my bathroom medicine cabinet. I found I almost never forgot to put it on, and it became a nightly habit fairly quickly. *Make it obvious.*

Have you ever made walking dates with your best friend? You might want to get in the habit of walking more but can't seem to motivate yourself to do it. You love talking to your best friend. The walk becomes far more attractive when paired with thirty minutes of uninterrupted time with your best gal pal. *Make it attractive.*

My kids were in a bad habit of scrounging for snacks right before dinner. They would go into the pantry and dig around for carb-filled snacks. This habit was getting in the way of them finishing their dinner and eating healthy options. I decided to start putting veggies with dip or cut up fruit on the table as an "appetizer." When they started to rummage, I would point them in the direction of the colorful, ready-to-eat snacks. *Make it easy.*

Do you love checking things off a list or a tracker? I truly love nothing more. When writing this book, in order to meet my tight deadline, I needed to write every day. If I missed a day, it would make it very difficult to catch up. Since I was not in the habit of writing daily at that point, I needed a way to keep myself on track. I created a writing tracker and put "write" with a little checkbox on my planner every day. Every day I would write, I got to check that box. *Make it satisfying.*

You can use the reverse of these tactics to break a bad habit, per James Clear. Let's look at how this can work in practice.

When I started eating better and wanted to change the habits of my family, I knew we needed a complete kitchen reorganization. There was no way for us to keep healthy eating habits if there were chips in the pantry and ice cream in the freezer. We cleaned those things out and only buy them when we plan for them, like Friday night pizza and ice cream night. *Make it invisible.*

In Chapter 9, we talk about how the people you surround yourself with can impact your motivation and energy. The same is true for habits. If you hang out with people that hate their jobs, eat fast food all the time, and let their kids do whatever they want, chances are you might find those things to be acceptable. What if you are hoping to make a behavior change like cooking dinner every night instead of ordering takeout? You could join a group or find a friend who also prioritizes cooking over junk. They would think it gross to eat fast food nightly. *Make it unattractive.*

I wanted to break a painfully bad habit of checking my phone. During the workday, I found myself checking it even when it didn't ring. When working on a hard task or just needing a break, I found myself picking up my phone without even thinking about it. This was becoming a time-waster and a distraction. Instead of keeping my phone charging in my home office, I plugged it in my upstairs bathroom. In order to check my phone, I would have to leave my office and go upstairs to the bathroom which was far less convenient. *Make it difficult.*

We have all heard the story of the kid who was caught smoking. Instead of punishing the child, the dad said, "You can smoke, but you have to smoke the whole pack." Gross. Giving a habit a painful or unwanted consequence lessens the likelihood of continuing the behavior. *Make it unsatisfying.*

USE HABIT STACKING

Habit stacking is adding a new, wanted habit to something you already do habitually. You might have seen this example when people want to add movement to their day. They decide to do squats while they brush their teeth or they do crunches on the kitchen floor while they heat up their coffee for the twenty-seventh time that day.

To use habit stacking, you take a habit that is already ritualized, like brushing your teeth or reheating your coffee, and add a wanted activity, like moving your body.

Think about where you could add habit stacking to your life.

- What habits do you do every day?
- What good habits are you trying to add to your life?
- How could you combine these for the most effective result?

SMALL CHANGES BECOME BIG CHANGES

Before I had developed a solid exercise habit, I never wore tennis shoes unless I was working out. Living in Phoenix, I have the privilege to wear flip-flops nearly year-round. I wore flip-flops, dress shoes, and cute flats but never tennis shoes.

I even had a friend say to me one day at school pick up, "I never see you in workout clothes!" I was dressed in running shoes and full workout gear, because I had actually worked out that day.

"I only wear workout clothes when I work out. Unfortunately, that is not very often!" I laughed.

When I would want to work out, but really did not feel like it, I would put on my tennis shoes. I knew that, in my mind, "you only wear tennis shoes when you work out." I might have not felt like working out, but once my shoes were on, I felt obligated to at least take a walk or do a quick video. You only wear tennis shoes when you work out.

I only required myself to put on my shoes, but that one small change meant I got in some movement for the day.

Stanford behavior change researcher B.J. Fogg confirms, "To create a new habit, you must first simplify the behavior. Make it tiny, even ridiculous. A good tiny behavior is easy to do—and fast."[6]

In his book *Tiny Habits: The Small Changes that Change Everything*, he talks about flossing one tooth, doing one pushup, and reading one sentence in a book to avoid relying on motivation and to instead focus on creating the habit. Putting on my shoes was easy and fast. Taking a 30-minute walk required far more motivation. By putting on my shoes, though, I ignited the motivation to get the walk in for the day.

———————————

SUPERMOM SHORTCUT•THE SECRET OF HABITS • CHAPTER WRAP UP

WHAT WE LEARNED

Habits are the basic building blocks of keeping it together as a supermom. Systems and routines become habits and make it much easier to devote energy and time to things that matter. Fortifying good habits and squashing bad habits are sure ways to help you be successful in all other areas of life. There is no true supermom who doesn't have solid habits.

HOW WE APPLY IT

There are a multitude of strategies for creating good habits and extinguishing bad habits. In this chapter, we covered:

- Stop Changing Processes: By setting routines, you give yourself the chance to create habits to do tasks faster and with less mental energy.
- Evaluate Your Habit Loops: The habit loop starts with a cue, which follows a routine, and gives you a reward. Evaluate where you can make a change to get the same reward with a new cue or routine.
- Use James Clear's Four Laws: If you want to start a habit, make it obvious, attractive, easy, and satisfying. If you

want to stop a bad habit, make it invisible, unattractive, difficult, and unsatisfying.

- Use Habit Stacking: Think of a good habit you already have in place, like driving the same route or brushing your teeth. Determine how you can add another good habit to that routine or "stack" the habits.
- Small Changes Become Big Changes: Make a small, extraordinarily easy change to get a habit in place. Doing so will help the desired habit unfold naturally.

ONE SMALL STEP

Pick one behavior you would like to change and create one small step to get there. Do you want to work out every morning? Every morning, put on your running shoes. Do you want to drink more water? Every morning, drink just one cup.

WHAT COMES NEXT

In the next chapter, we talk about another of the most important secrets to becoming a supermom: confidence. Without confidence, you are likely to procrastinate, second-guess yourself, become jealous of others, and self-sabotage. A healthy self-esteem is a key to success at work and home.

CHAPTER 2
SUPERMOMS BELIEVE THEY ARE AMAZING

THE SECRET OF CONFIDENCE

"It is confidence in our bodies, minds and spirits that allows us to keep looking for new adventures, new directions to grow in, and new lessons to learn, which is what life is all about."
—Oprah Winfrey, *O, The Oprah Magazine*[7]

"It is our light, not our darkness that most frightens us. We ask ourselves, 'Who am I to be brilliant, gorgeous, talented, fabulous?' Actually, who are you not to be?... Your playing small does not serve the world. There is nothing enlightened about shrinking so that other people won't feel insecure around you."
—Marianne Williamson, *A Return to Love* [8]

Confidence can be tricky. We go about life thinking, "Sure, I have confidence. I am a self-confident person."

Then we find ourselves jealous of our friends. We find ourselves caring what everyone else will say or what everyone else will think. We think people are talking behind our backs. We compare ourselves to others. We say yes to things we absolutely don't want to do because we don't want people to think badly about us. We find ourselves people-pleasing but resentful.

Confidence is defined as "a feeling of self-assurance arising from one's appreciation of one's own abilities or qualities"[9] and "a belief in your own ability to do things and be successful."[10]

It isn't about just feeling good in your skin. It isn't about being skinny or beautiful. Confidence is a deep-set belief that you will be able to do new things, learn new processes, and consistently become better.

THE ENEMIES OF CONFIDENCE

A few things can quickly deteriorate your level of confidence: comparison, jealousy, and people-pleasing.

COMPARISON

What other people are doing is none of your business. It has absolutely nothing to do with you. Stop comparing your abilities, talents, possessions, and life to everyone else.

What happens when we compare ourselves to others? When you compare, you are focusing on the other person instead of focusing on yourself. Instead of taking all of your energy and putting it toward your own goals, you are wasting energy on what others are doing.

Comparing can erode confidence because there will always be someone smarter, someone happier, someone richer, someone with a nicer house, someone with a faster promotion schedule, someone with a faster growing business. If you look for them, you can find them. You *will* find them. They are not the point.

You don't even know if their life actually is better. They may pretend to be happy but be miserable. They may pretend to have a lot of money but be heavily in debt.

What if they actually are unbelievably rich and happy? Does that somehow make your life worse? It doesn't.

This is where the benefit of a gratitude practice comes in. Gratitude teaches you to focus on what you do have instead of what you don't. It teaches you to look at your life and stop looking at everyone else.

JEALOUSY

What other people have is none of your business. The evil twin of comparison is jealousy. Jealousy takes comparison to the next level. Not only are you focusing on other people, but now you want what they have. Jealousy can lead to some pretty unfavorable belief patterns.

Jealous of your favorite co-worker's promotion?

"She only got promoted because the V.P. likes her better than anyone else."

Instead of conceding that she actually is amazing at her job, you are pretending that her promotion was unwarranted. Instead of focusing on what you can do better to obtain a similar promotion, if you want it, you are denouncing her and talking behind her back.

Jealousy can cause you to feel insecure and resentful leading to suspicions, insults, and discouragement. Someone else's successes, in any area, say nothing about yours. Other people's possessions say nothing about you. If you are finding yourself lost in jealousy or spending more time with people that are also jealous, it's time to rethink thought patterns and associates.

PEOPLE-PLEASING

What other people think about you is none of your business. It really isn't.

We all want people to like us. We want to be loved and cherished. We want people to like to be around us, to feel good in our presence.

This means that you should be nice and honest and trustworthy. You should be caring and responsible and a good friend. You should not do things because that is what you think other people want. You should not fully sacrifice yourself to make other people happy. Being a martyr will only drain your energy and your confidence.

A NOTE ABOUT NARCISSISM

There is a wild difference between confidence and narcissism. Confidence is an internal belief that you are smart, competent, and able to figure things out. Because of this belief, you are able to place your focus away from yourself to help and support others. You do not require affirmation from others and can step back to see where your competence is valid and where you need to improve your skills.

Narcissism is being absorbed with yourself and thinking you are more important and better than other people. At the same time, narcissists need constant reassurance and affirmation from others, exploit their relationships, and rarely admit fault. We are looking to build confidence from success, not narcissism.

BUILDING YOUR CONFIDENT SELF

Along with habits, confidence is another critical starting point to being a supermom. Without a certain level of confidence, you can never grow to your full potential. You can never be the best possible *you*.

MINDSET: BELIEVING YOU ARE AMAZING

An important part of confidence and a growth mindset is believing that you are capable of anything. Trusting that you are able to take any opportunity, any adversity and any mistake, and come through on the other side better is confidence. Believing that you are everything you can be, not better than anyone else, but the best you is the path to self-esteem.

BELIEVING THAT YOU ARE EVERYTHING YOU CAN BE, NOT BETTER THAN ANYONE ELSE, BUT THE BEST YOU IS THE PATH TO SELF-ESTEEM.

AFFIRMATIONS

You might have heard about affirmations. You might already use them. You might think they are *woo-woo*. Either way, positive affirmations are a proven way to change the way you think. A positive affirmation is a positive statement that you repeat over and over, often aloud, to challenge negative and self-sabotaging thoughts.

Some examples of affirmations you might try out are:

- My mind is open, and I am ready to lead.
- I live in abundance and know great things will come to me.
- I am a confident and self-aware person.
- I appreciate the value in everyone and am valued in return.
- I am perfect the way that I am.
- I create my own happiness.
- I am enough.
- _____
- _____
- _____
- _____
- _____
- _____

Think about the person you want to be, and write down a few positive affirmations you can repeat on a daily basis. Write them on a piece of paper or in your workbook. You could even work these into your morning or evening routine.

MANTRAS

Similar to an affirmation in practice, a mantra is usually one word and often associated with prayer or meditation. The goal is similar, however, in that you are focusing on becoming the word you have in your mind. You may use peace, relax, or release as your word as you focus in meditation or prayer.

In Chapter 10, we talk about the importance of rest and review some great breathing exercises that can help you feel less stressed. Using a mantra during this time can help you focus on being relaxed *and* confident.

BE BRAVE

Taking risks is scary. As moms that want it all, we have to be willing to take risks and be brave. The only way we will get to the heights of our career and our motherhood is by digging deep and finding that courage to move forward despite adversity or failure.

As brave and confident adults, we can raise brave and confident children. Carol S. Dweck, author of *Mindset: The New Psychology of Success*, said, "Parents think they can hand children permanent confidence—like a gift—by praising their brains and talent. It doesn't work, and in fact has the opposite effect. It makes children doubt themselves as soon as anything is hard or anything goes wrong. If parents want to give their children a gift, the best thing they can do is to teach their children to love challenges, be intrigued by mistakes, enjoy effort, and keep on learning. That way, their children don't have to be slaves of praise. They will have a lifelong way to build and repair their own confidence."[11]

SUPERMOM SHORTCUT • THE SECRET OF CONFIDENCE • CHAPTER WRAP UP

WHAT WE LEARNED

Self-esteem is a critical component to success in parenting, friendships, relationships, and work. When you do not feel confident, you are more likely to compare yourself to others, act out of jealousy, and people-please.

HOW WE APPLY IT

In order to increase confidence and decrease feelings of jealousy or comparison, the following tactics can be used:

- Mindset: Believe you are Amazing: Working on your growth mindset can help you believe that you are capable of anything.
- Affirmations: Positive affirmations are positive statements that you repeat every day to remind yourself of the person that you are and the person you want to be.
- Mantras: Mantras can be used during prayer, meditation, or breathing exercises. You think the same word repeatedly to remind yourself of the feeling you want in your life.

- Be Brave: You must be able to summon the courage to push through challenges or adversities to come out more confident on the other side.

ONE SMALL STEP

Make a list of positive affirmations that you could say about yourself. Pick one and say it every morning as part of your morning routine.

WHAT COMES NEXT

In the next chapter, we review another key to supermom success. High-performing moms know the importance of morning routines. When you can conquer your morning, you set yourself up for a day of success.

CHAPTER 3
SUPERMOMS WIN THE DAY

THE SECRET OF MORNING ROUTINES

"How you wake up each day and your morning routine (or lack thereof) dramatically affects your levels of success in every single area of your life. Focused, productive, successful mornings generate focused, productive, successful days which inevitably create a successful life in the same way that unfocused, unproductive, and mediocre mornings generate unfocused, unproductive, and mediocre days, and ultimately a mediocre quality of life. By simply changing the way you wake up in the morning, you can transform any area of your life, faster than you ever thought possible."

—Hal Elrod, *The Miracle Morning: The Not-So-Obvious Secret Guaranteed to Transform Your Life (Before 8AM)*[12]

"I have always been delighted at the prospect of a new day, a fresh try, one more start, with perhaps a bit of magic waiting somewhere behind the morning."

—J. B. Priestley[13]

"**M**ommy, are you awake?"

Groggy and already irritated by the tiny voice mere inches from her face, she opened her eyes.

"I'm hungry."

Amber looked at the clock. It was already 6:30 a.m. Crap. They had to leave at 7:30 a.m. if she was going to drop off every child and get to work by 9:00 a.m. She had not showered. No one had eaten. It was going to be another morning filled with rushing, likely a lot of yelling, and struggling to get in the car on time. There would be lost shoes and missed homework.

Someone would cry. Usually a kid, but sometimes Amber. Everyone would be angry by the time they were dropped at school and daycare, then she would take deep breaths in her car before she stepped out to tackle an intense work day.

Can you relate?

So many of us start the day and allow it to control us. We bend to the immediate pressures. We are unfocused. We are *tired*.

To fix this, you need a clear morning routine to make sure your day does not start out of your control. Tim Ferriss, the author of *The 4-Hour Workweek*[14] among other great books on productivity, says that if you win the morning, you will win the day. I think there is nothing closer to the truth.

A morning with you in control ensures your day unfolds in the exact way you intend. No one wants to start a day unfocused, out of control, and without a plan.

You might be saying to yourself, but I am not a "morning person." No one is asking you to run a 10K at 5:00 a.m. No one is saying you need to wake up with some sort of Mary Poppins-level happiness.

What I am saying is that you have very little chance of having a day that you can feel proud of if you don't start it strong. What I am telling you is if you fail to plan your day, you essentially plan to fail it.

This concept is not revolutionary. Morning routines have been big in the news. You can find entire books on the topic. You can dive deep and get very strict on your plan for the morning, if you choose to do that. As a busy career mom who already wakes up at 4:00 a.m., I am very serious about my morning. I want to include only the compulsory tasks and nothing that won't move the needle of my day. I want every minute to matter.

Before we dive into the components that I think are a must for a morning that wins the day, I want to be clear: you do not need to wake up at 4:00 a.m. You do not need to work out for an hour. You do not need to be happy to start a routine.

But...you do need to start your day with a plan. You need to at least try it. I know it will change your productivity and your overall happiness. I know this because hundreds of succeeding moms are doing it. I believe it will change your life.

———————

What is a morning routine? What does that even mean? A morning routine is a list of activities that you do every day, or almost every day, to set you up for a spectacular day. A clear morning routine is a strategy session of sorts, with yourself, to make sure you have a plan for the day and are ready to take it on with strength and energy. It is a time to focus on you.

If you are waking up with your kids, you are already on the wrong side of the day. Do not do this. Sleeping babies are little cherubs. Those little angels wake up and then need something constantly.

"Mom, I'm hungry."

"Mom, where are my shoes?"

"Mom, Kaden won't get out of my room!"

"Mom, I can't find my homework!"

"Mom, why don't I have any clean underwear?"

"Mom, do I have to bring my trumpet today?"

Parents, especially moms, cannot start their day with their children. You just can't. I don't care if you are not a morning person. You need at least a few minutes to ready yourself to be the mom, the businesswoman, and the human you know you can be. You deserve it.

A mere twenty minutes can give you the time you need to own the day. Can you wake up an hour before the rest of the family? Even better.

I have critical parts of my morning, and things I add in when I can. You will structure your morning for you. Let's start with the non-negotiables, for me.

> IF YOU ARE WAKING UP WITH YOUR KIDS, YOU ARE ALREADY ON THE WRONG SIDE OF THE DAY.

COFFEE

Don't judge, friends. I start every single day with a cup of coffee.

The beans are roasted right in my backyard at the hands of my talented husband. They are a perfect City + Roast. (He has become a coffee snob. I don't ask questions.) They are freshly ground and make the best cup of coffee you have ever had in your life.

I drink it black. You can drink it cold, and it still tastes amazing. It is never bitter. It does not give you jitters. It is pure heaven.

I could write a sales page about this coffee.

It is low in caffeine, so it is not about the energy it gives me or the need to "wake up." It is simply about taking a few sips to enjoy the perfection of the delicious, hot coffee in a dark and quiet house. And, then, I get to planning!

Hate coffee, tea, water? Just skip this one.

PLAN THE DAY

We dive deeper into time management, productivity, and planning in Chapters 13 and 14 and discuss planning for your week or your month, even your year. The most critical component of my morning routine is a plan for the *day*.

Whether you use a day planner, a calendar, a digital planner, or another favorite time-management tool, you need to know what you are doing to do it well. Seventy percent of the successful moms I surveyed used a time-management tool and ongoing lists to keep themselves organized.

I have had moms argue that you should plan an entire week or that you should plan at night instead of the morning. I think that we work best when we say, "This is what I am going to do." Then, we do it.

I use that exact strategy in the morning. I review my planner for the day and detail what I am going to do. Then, I start.

The most important thing about planning is that it comes *first*. Not after you check your emails, not after you grab your phone for a quick social media post. You can do those things, but you will plan for them and not allow them to start your day on a runaway train.

YOUR ONE THING

I love the book *The One Thing* by Gary Keller and Jay Papasan.[15] In the book, they detail why you need to focus on one thing in any given area of your life: the one thing that will make "everything else easier or even unnecessary." You pick your most important goal and you focus the next best step to get to the finish line.

When you are planning your day, think about the one thing that would make your day a success. Is it a killer presentation for your team? Is it making the most amazing cake for your oldest child's eighth birthday? Is it winning over the client who seems a little bit on the fence? Is it getting in your workout no matter what?

Now, look at your plan for your day. Look at the actual schedule for what is going to happen. Do you see that one most important goal? Is there time blocked for it? Can you make it happen?

If not, consider shifting your day around. What can wait until tomorrow? What is a "nice-to-have" in your day instead of a "need-to-have"? What can you deprioritize for today to prioritize the most important goal? Do you struggle with priorities? Supermoms know that setting priorities is a critical skill—more on that in Chapter 12.

GRATITUDE

Honestly, gratitude might deserve its own chapter. Over the years, research has shown that the feeling and display of gratitude is critical to mindset, attitude, and overall happiness. Gratitude is a key secret to making the best of your every day.

Later in the book, we talk more about attitude and how that can change the way we take on challenges, succeed in activities, and feel about the people around us. Research shows that starting our day in an attitude of gratitude allows improved optimism, increased happiness, lower stress and stronger self-control.[16] Every one of these qualities leads us to a better, happier, and more fulfilled life.

I start my day writing down something I am grateful for that day. Although I am certainly grateful for my career, my house, my family, and my health, these are not the things I write down each morning.

I get *very specific*. I write something particular that I am thankful for in that exact moment on that exact day. I bring myself back to the precise moment where I had that feeling of gratitude, and I let myself feel it again. This helps me to embody that attitude of gratitude I am trying to foster for my morning.

Here are some examples of things I have written over the past year:

- I am grateful that Kaden walked up and gave me one last hug before he went outside to play and said, "I love you Mommy."
- I am grateful that my friend Traci invited me to participate in her "presents for seniors" campaign.
- I am grateful that I had an honest and open conversation with Rebecca (my client) for our weekly touch base.
- I am grateful that everyone loved dinner last night, and everyone said thank you without being asked. (Mom win!)
- I am grateful for the stories Kellen told me about his day on the way home from preschool.

There is one more thing I love to do with my gratitude, and that is to *share it*. An attitude of gratitude can certainly be created just by being grateful. Feeling thankful on the inside is the first step. A great way to increase feelings of positivity is to share that gratitude with others.

Who doesn't like hearing "thanks," or "I appreciate you," or "you make me happy"? If I am feeling grateful as a result of someone else, I tell them. If I am feeling positively toward someone, I tell them. A quick note, email, voice text, text message… anything will do the trick to help the recipient feel the positivity you have created within too.

EXERCISE AND MEAL PLANNING

Those of you that don't struggle keeping your workout or making healthy choices, I applaud your self-control and willpower. I am not that girl.

We talk in this book about health, exercise, food choices and energy. We know that these things are wildly connected. If we are not taking care of our bodies, then we cannot be the best anything, not the best in our career and not the best parent. They are necessary, but sometimes they are just plain hard.

Planning my exercise and food for the day gives me a better chance of making the right choices. I am not starving and trying to decide what to order for lunch. Spoiler alert—it will be an overload of chips and guacamole or a cheese-filled sandwich every time. I am not *hoping* to get in my workout for the day. I am not trying to decide what to make for dinner at 6:00 p.m.

It also reminds me about food planning for my family. Although Jeremy cooks occasionally—when he has to because I am not home—I am mostly responsible for cooking. He is responsible for cleaning—again, when we are both home.

Sometimes I need to put out some ground chicken to thaw. Sometimes I need to make the kids' lunches or breakfasts. Sometimes I need longer to prep a meal and might need to make a last-minute shift due to an unexpected department meeting or conference with a teacher.

Reviewing planned food and movement in the morning allows me to avoid eleventh-hour scrambling, unwanted energy dips, and frustration at the end of the day.

That's it! This only takes me twenty or thirty minutes at the most, and then I head out for my workout (most days) or otherwise get my day started. Even when the tiny humans have awoken early (again, most days) and are ready to rock at 5:00 a.m., I have already won the day.

SUPERMOM SHORTCUT • THE SECRET OF MORNING ROUTINES • CHAPTER WRAP UP

WHAT WE LEARNED

When you allow your day to start in a flurry of whining children, rushing around, and overall chaos, you set yourself up to fail. Creating a consistent and easy morning routine is the very best way to win the day.

HOW WE APPLY IT

Create a plan for your day incorporating the following:

- Coffee (optional), but for me, hot coffee is a perfect start to my quiet morning in my quiet house.
- Use your calendar or planner to plan the whole day. Time block where needed and ensure all responsibilities have a scheduled time to be completed.
- Determine your one big goal for the day and make sure it has a premier place in your schedule.

- Incorporate a gratitude practice writing down specific things you are thankful for in that most recent day. Then, if you have extra time, share that thanks with someone else in a quick email or text.
- Plan your food and movement goal for the day so you can maintain energy and focus.

ONE SMALL STEP

Tomorrow—yes, tomorrow—set your alarm for five minutes earlier than you usually get up. Put your alarm or your phone across the room and force yourself to get up just five minutes earlier. Try to add in a few minutes each day and replace it with one of the strategies above. It will change your life.

WHAT COMES NEXT

In the next chapter, we will talk about the last of the key secrets of supermom: the secret of help. No one can do everything by herself and stay happy and productive. Supermoms know that help is one of the most important keys to success.

CHAPTER 4
SUPERMOMS DON'T DO IT ALL

THE SECRET OF HELP

"If you want to do a few small things right, do them yourself. If you want to do great things and make a big impact, learn to delegate."

— John C. Maxwell[17]

"Ask for help not because you are weak but because you want to remain strong."

— Les Brown[18]

She walked into the conference room with bags under her eyes and her left pant leg wrinkled. Her laptop cable was partially hanging out of her computer bag.

"Did you just get in?" I asked her.

"No, I got in around 3:00 a.m. I am so tired."

"I thought you were driving in last night. What happened?"

"I had to stay home until I made all the meals for the week. I didn't get on the road until way later than I had planned."

"Wait, what!?!"

We were in Austin for a team meeting, and people were flying and driving in from all over the United States. Gabby was lucky enough to live within driving distance, but it was still about three hours from her Dallas suburb.

She went on to tell me that her husband didn't really know how to cook, so she made meals for every night of the week before she left for the business trip. She had also laid out all the kid's outfits, put the dog food in pre-made bags, and pre-printed all the homework assignments.

"He is an adult, right?" I teased. I sort of wasn't kidding.

Instead of delegating some of these tasks to her husband while she was gone or asking for help, she did them all herself. It left her with barely any sleep and limited brainpower for a team meeting that expected high energy. By not asking for help, she put her role on the team in jeopardy.

Being a supermom isn't about doing it all. It isn't about being perfect. It is about doing all the things that actually matter. It is about asking for help so you can do just that.

This can be *really hard* for supermoms.

As high-performing creatures, we tend to be controlling. Letting go of control can be challenging. We want things done *our way* on *our schedule*. We think we are the only ones that can really do it right.

The truth is that you will never become the highest performing in your home and career if you don't learn how to ask for help. When you delegate the things that are less important, you free up time to focus on the bigger goals and the bigger dreams. You give yourself time to focus on the true priorities.

Four years ago, I finally agreed to hire a company to clean our house every two weeks. My husband had tried to convince me *for years* that we needed a house cleaner. For years, I declined.

"It's too expensive. I could do so many other things with that money."

"Cleaning house isn't hard. We can just do it ourselves."

"We will have to be out of the house for hours. When could we even do that?"

All of these things were just excuses. Instead, I would fight with him every week over who did what, and who was not helping. This was not good for our kids or our marriage. Finally, he convinced me with this.

THE TRUTH IS THAT YOU WILL NEVER BECOME THE HIGHEST PERFORMING IN YOUR HOME AND CAREER IF YOU DON'T LEARN HOW TO ASK FOR HELP.

"How long would you say it takes you to clean the house every weekend?" he asked one week.

"Well, it takes less time with help, but probably three hours or so," I responded honestly, albeit with a passive-aggressive dig.

"Wouldn't you rather spend three hours with the kids doing something fun on the weekend?"

Whoa.

Yes, 1000%, yes! I would love to have more time to go to the zoo or the park. I would love to have more time for picnics and bike rides and baking cupcakes.

That week we scheduled with a service and never looked back. It doesn't mean I don't have to clean at all. With six humans and two giant dogs in this house, things can get tornado-like pretty quickly. What it does give me is time to watch a movie with the kids instead of scrub toilets.

I was always bad at delegating and asking for help even when I was a child. Being completely independent was a badge of honor. I still have that badge, and sometimes it is shining bright to this day. However, this small change at home helped me realize that I could be doing bigger and better things if I relinquished control. I was still strong and independent if I let people help me. I might even be better at the important things if I outsourced the less important.

Over the years, I have learned some reliable tips that make asking for help, delegating, and outsourcing easier and more effective. Teamwork really does make the dream work.

HOW TO ASK FOR HELP

Have you ever gone over to a friend's house for a dinner party? You walk in the front door, hand them a bottle of wine, and ask what you can do to help. They say, "Oh, nothing, I've got it!" Meanwhile they are running around the kitchen like a chicken with its head cut off, rushing from countertop to countertop, pan to pan, to make sure nothing goes awry.

The sad thing here is that you actually wanted to help. You weren't just offering to be nice. It feels good to help other people. It feels good to be needed and useful. She could have been less stressed, and you would have a nice little boost of dopamine for helping your friend.

My friend Jess is great at asking for help. If you walk into her house for a party, she puts you to straight to work. One person is lining up champagne glasses, another is chopping cucumbers, and another is peeling potatoes. Everyone is in the kitchen talking and laughing and drinking and having a fantastic time. Many hands make light work—and more fun.

How do some people ask for help so readily while others struggle? Simply put, we don't want to be vulnerable. We think that asking for help makes us weak or less than. How dare we show someone that we can't manage everything?

We also don't want to lose control. Particularly for those Type A moms, the idea of giving someone else control over any part of our life is stressful, even something as small as grocery shopping or carpooling the kids to football practice.

What are some ways that we can make asking for help easier? First, remember that people like to help. As humans, we like to give to other people. Why? It is biological. Helping others gives us a physical reaction that increases oxytocin, serotonin, and dopamine. It literally makes our brain happier.

It is important to remember that people like to help, but they don't like to be taken advantage of. Asking for help should never look like manipulation, abusing a friendship, or an attack.

BE VULNERABLE

It is okay to need help. It is okay to ask for help. It is okay to tell someone you can't do it all. It is okay not to do it all. It is okay to be vulnerable.

When you are asking for help at work or at home, it is okay to say, "I am drowning. Can you help me?"

BE PRECISE

When you are asking for help, be clear and precise about exactly what it is you are asking. Your intent is not to be controlling but to be very clear where help is needed. It allows you to ensure the other person understands where you are asking for help. It also allows them to decide if they can, indeed, provide the help you are requesting.

Let's pretend you are at work and creating a slide presentation. Your content is ready, but you are inexperienced with creating PowerPoint slides with animations. You know that Bill is *amazing* at PowerPoint.

Instead of, "Hey, Bill, do you think you could help me with some slides?" a more precise request would be, "Hey, Bill! I am really struggling with the animations for our PowerPoint presentation. I have five slides that need animations, and I just can't seem to get them to work. Do you think you could help me tomorrow?"

The precise request is better because Bill knows exactly what you are asking and can decide if he has available time to complete this request. Clear communication also ensures both people are on the same page with the same expectations.

DON'T ASK FOR A LITTLE, THEN TAKE A LOT

People do not like to be manipulated, swindled, or taken advantage of. Another reason you want to be very precise when you are asking for help is to prevent this feeling for people you care about.

Your friend doesn't want to agree to drop you off at a doctor's appointment only to realize that she will also be waiting forty-five minutes for you and taking you back home afterward.

He peeks his head around my doorframe.

"Hey, Lori, do you think you could help me? It won't take more than a minute of your time."

"Umm…sure…as long as it is fast."

He proceeds to go through a twenty-page report with flagrant errors and starts berating the author. His face is turning red and voice is getting louder. He is clearly frustrated.

I want to help. I want to go through every page with him, help him calm down, and support him through his frustrating moment.

But. He said a minute. *One* minute. This was apt to take at least thirty.

This is a great example of a terrible time-waster we talk about later in this book. As you make an effort to avoid time-wasters in your own day, don't be that time-waster for someone else.

DON'T APOLOGIZE

When you are asking someone to help you, just ask. Be vulnerable and ask. Don't say you are sorry over and over again. Don't say how you should be able to do this yourself. Don't point to how stupid you are for needing help.

Not only does this make your helper very uncomfortable in the moment, but it ensures they will never ask for your help. After all, you would think how dumb and incompetent they are, wouldn't you?

HOW TO DELEGATE

What is the difference between asking for help and delegating? In this chapter, I am differentiating asking for help and delegation by this: leadership. You are in a position of leadership. When you are delegating, there is some level of hierarchy involved. For example, you may ask your boss for help but you can delegate to your team. You might ask your friend for help but delegate to your children.

Delegating is a critical skill for business and home leaders. Critical. You will never be able to do everything. You do not need to jeopardize your sleep, your health, or your relationships to do everything yourself. Delegation is key.

Before we talk about how to delegate, I want to discuss delegation versus dumping. Dumping is taking all your crappiest tasks and giving them to someone else on your team or in your home. They don't benefit the recipient and only serve to benefit you.

Delegation, on the other hand, is eliminating a task on your plate while giving someone else the opportunity to learn a new task, have a new responsibility, or grow in some way.

Chores for your children can be an example of delegating house duties. Your children are learning responsibility, how to actually do whatever task they are assigned, and financial management if you are paying them to complete chores.

How do you delegate without dumping?

LET GO

Stop hoarding all the work. Stop thinking only you can do everything. Stop believing you are a unicorn in a world of horses. Your kids can learn to fold towels the "right" way. Your assistant can learn to prepare the meeting agenda. Your team can put together the presentation.

You have to learn to let go of control if you really want to delegate well. You have to learn to trust your team and your family. Delegating doesn't free up your time for the bigger and better tasks if you are constantly hovering and following up on every detail.

USE THEIR STRENGTHS

When you think of the person you want to delegate to, what strengths come to mind? Are they great talking to clients? Are they super detail-oriented? Are they a great editor and can always find the mistakes in a sales presentation?

If you focus on the areas where your team member is already strong, you can tailor the responsibilities you delegate to grow and develop those skills even more.

TEACH NEW SKILLS

You can also use delegation to teach a new skill. I had a team member that had never worked on a client proposal. In order for her to be eligible for her next promotion, she had to have that skill and experience. Knowing this information, I was able to delegate a big section of our next proposal to her and provide support through the process.

Removing tasks from our long list of things to do cannot only benefit us, but can benefit those that need to gain the experience we already have under our belt.

For our kids, this might look like teaching a house or life skill. When I was in college, I was a Resident Assistant (RA). I lived in a dorm on campus to support freshman students. I can't tell you how many eighteen-year-old students didn't know how to do laundry. They didn't know how to clean their bathrooms or how to microwave macaroni & cheese. Skills learned at home allow greater success when they leave your house, even if that only means not dying all their underwear pink with their new red T-shirt.

INTRODUCE FEEDBACK LOOPS

You should not hover, but you should have a way to gauge progress and ensure quality. Feedback loops are a great way to monitor an activity without being integrated into every detail.

A feedback loop is a method of obtaining feedback on a regular interval or at a specific stage.

My son, Kaden, wanted to earn extra money and offered to vacuum out my car. This was typically my job, so I was happy to delegate. He had never vacuumed it before, and I wasn't sure he would be the most detail-oriented.

Instead of having him vacuum the whole car and have me come check it, I had him vacuum just the front row. He came to get me after that row, and I was able to show him where he missed spots, better technique at holding the hose, and how to move the floor mats.

Setting up this feedback loop allowed him to improve on the second row and need no correction on the third row. Although a simple example, this clearly shows the benefit of feedback loops.

HOW TO OUTSOURCE

Outsourcing is paying someone outside of your home or office to complete an assigned task or expectation. At our house, housecleaning is outsourced. Landscaping maintenance is outsourced. Annual taxes are outsourced.

Think about how you may already be using outsourcing and not even realize it. Do you have a day care provider, babysitter, nanny, window cleaner, dog walker, or house sitter? Do you pay someone to paint your toenails? Yes, even a pedicure can be outsourcing. You could do it yourself, but you pay someone else to do it better.

Depending on your career, outsourcing may or may not be an option for you. If you own your own business, it is essential. You cannot be amazing at everything and need to play to your strengths. You do the things that make your business move and where you are highly skilled. You outsource what you are not as good at doing (website design?), what takes more time than it is worth (managing and tracking receipts?), or that you simply don't like to do (taxes?).

Even if you work for a larger company, think about where there may be room for outsourcing. Are you spending more time or money than necessary in a certain area? Could you decrease cost and increase efficiency by proposing a new strategy?

When you decide that a responsibility can be outsourced, keep these things in mind.

DEFINE THE SCOPE

You need to decide exactly what you need. What is the scope of the job you want done?

Let's say you are hiring a house cleaner. You want them to clean every room in your house, wash your windows and baseboards, wipe your ceiling fans, the works. Without a clear scope, your vendor cannot accurately predict the time and effort it will take to get the job done.

CHOOSE BASED ON EXPERIENCE AND COST, NOT JUST PRICE

Whether you are hiring an assistant, choosing a landscaper, or picking a daycare, ask the right questions to know they will do the job right. Cheaper is not always better if you might have to do the job again or provide so much guidance that the time is not actually saved.

SIGN A CONTRACT

If it isn't in writing, it didn't happen. In order to protect yourself as well as the company or person that you are using for the job, always have a contract. It doesn't have to be fancy, but it does need to be in writing.

SUPERMOM SHORTCUT • THE SECRET OF HELP • CHAPTER WRAP UP

WHAT WE LEARNED

Supermoms, although they appear to do it all, definitely don't. They know the priorities of their lives and use these priorities to make precise decisions on how things get done. They know the importance of asking for help, delegating to others, and outsourcing where possible.

HOW WE APPLY IT

Where in your life are you task hoarding? Where are you not asking for help and should? What are you doing that someone else could do to free you to focus on the bigger dreams and the brighter goals?

If you decide to ask for help, keep these things in mind:

- Be vulnerable: It is okay to say you can't do it all.
- Be precise: Ask for exactly what you need.
- Don't Ask for a Little, Then Take a Lot: Don't take advantage.
- Don't Apologize: Asking for help is not something to be sorry about.

The best delegators follow a few key strategies:

- Let Go: You can't keep full control and save the time you need to do bigger things.

- Use Their Strengths: Choose team members who have the skill you need to allow them to further develop.
- Teach New Skills: Help them develop new skills that you have already perfected.
- Introduce Feedback Loops: Set up a method of checks and balances to ensure quality.

Did you decide that outsourcing is the best way to get the job done? Don't forget:

- Define the Scope: Make sure you are clear on what job is to be done.
- Choose Based on Experience and Cost, Not Just Price: Although cost is an important factor, the cheapest cost is often the cheapest work.
- Sign a Contract: If it isn't in writing, it never happened.

ONE SMALL STEP

Decide one thing, right now, that you will stop doing in the next week. Decide who will do it instead whether you will ask someone to help you, delegate, or outsource.

Not going to strip the sheets off the beds and carry six loads of laundry downstairs anymore? Teach the kids to do it.

No longer creating your meeting agendas? Put time on the calendar to train your assistant.

Not going to grocery shop anymore? Schedule your delivery service.

WHAT COMES NEXT

In the next section, we will talk about the mind and body secrets to keep your health up, your energy high, and your mind clear. Without these qualities, you will struggle to maintain strength as supermom. We will start with physical health.

PART 2

SECRETS OF THE BODY AND MIND

CHAPTER 5
SUPERMOMS LOVE THEIR BODY

THE SECRET OF HEALTH

"To keep the body in good health is a duty, otherwise we shall not be able to keep our mind strong and clear."
— Buddha

"You cannot always control what goes on outside. But you can always control what goes on inside."
— Dr. Wayne Dyer

In June 2016, right as summer break from school kicked off for my three oldest children, I delivered my fourth and final baby. I had the ultimate luxury of taking twelve full weeks of maternity leave from my career, something I had never had the fortune to do with the other kids since much of it was unpaid. I wanted to make sure that the time I spent with my kids that summer was epic—a summer we would never forget. I wanted to make that time worth it. I knew so many moms that went through maternity leave in a blur. I was determined that would not be me.

We spent the summer going to our community pool nearly every day, reading books, using our annual pass to the Phoenix Zoo, visiting cousins, shopping, and eating popsicles. We had the best, most relaxing summer I had ever experienced as a mom. The kids were thrilled not to be in camp and to have a new baby in our house. I was thrilled just to be with them and to snuggle that baby every single day.

Then, August came.

In Phoenix, we start school in August instead of the typical post-Labor Day start date in most other parts of the country. The end of August also meant the return to work for me and likely the start of business travel.

My husband was traveling weekly for his job. The kids would be going to three different places each day: a home day care for baby Kellen, preschool for Kamryn, and elementary school for Kinley and Kaden. They would be starting flag football, musical theatre, and dance. I would have big deadlines and 6:00 a.m. meetings.

I needed something to guarantee that I would be superhuman to be able to manage all of the moving parts of work and family. I needed to be supermom.

Enter The Whole30®.

I had heard of the Whole30® meal plan from a friend nearly a year before this time. She had lost maybe ten pounds and had become much leaner. She said she felt great.

Then, she told me about the plan. No gluten, no sugar, no alcohol, no soy, no dairy.

Um, no, thank you. Restrictive diets were never for me. I knew that as soon as I stopped the diet, I wouldn't maintain any weight loss that I had achieved. I put it out of my mind as an option I would ever try.

The Whole30® appeared again for me that August, in a Facebook ad, but this time it had my attention. It wasn't talking about weight loss at all. It was talking about feeling your best, mental clarity, and peak performance. The program calls these "non-scale victories."[19] These non-scale victories sounded an awful lot like the supermom skills I needed to be my best. I was sold.

I signed up to do a September Whole30® and never looked back.

The beginning was hard. It was a pretty big shift from what I was eating, even though I was cooking relatively healthy meals already. I didn't feel great to start. The plan said that would be the case, and I trusted the process. I remained committed.

As the days continued on, I started to feel different. I had always been high energy, but I felt a level of energy like never before. I had always felt pretty sharp, but I felt a mental clarity like never before. I had always felt like I had it together, but I felt like a true supermom.

And I was *happy*, so stinking happy. Insides-bubbling-with-a-giggle-just-under-the-surface happy. Big-smile-on-my-face-for-no-reason happy. Happy is my sweet spot, it is the feeling I am striving for on a daily basis. To think that I could get genuine happiness by just changing the food I put in my body was mind-blowing. Life-changing.

The non-scale victories I experienced with this change in eating are too numerous to fully list, but let me share a few more:

- I was still nursing an infant who woke up multiple times a night. My sleep was so good between these nursing sessions that I could wake in the morning feeling refreshed with limited hours of sleep.
- My energy was consistent throughout the day and didn't dip dramatically in the afternoon.
- My mind felt like it was on fire! I felt like I could complete every task faster and better than I could in the past.
- My anxiety was gone. Although never diagnosed officially, I would often get a feeling like I was crawling out of my skin. With a history in counseling and education in marriage and family therapy, I knew this was anxiety. When I changed my eating habits, I no longer felt the urge to climb out of my body.
- I was more patient with the kids. I had always tried to be patient on the outside, even when my insides were boiling. The change in eating habits simmered the boil, so I didn't have to control the patience anymore. It just came.
- My skin was clear and kind of glowing. Think pregnancy without the actual baby.

The Whole30® meal plan is not intended to be a forever lifestyle nor is it a weight loss plan. At the end of 30 days, you reintroduce foods one by one to see what has the largest impact on your mind and body. Does dairy make your stomach bloat? Now you know. Does extra sugar zap your energy and affect your memory? Now you know. Does alcohol make you wake up at 2:00 a.m. or give you bad dreams? Now you know.

I am not a medical professional, and this is not *at all* a recommendation for everyone to try the Whole30®. (Although, I did convince quite a few friends and co-workers to try it with all the positive benefits I experienced.) There are plenty of eating plans that can give you similar results and can help you identify what might be affecting your body in a negative way.

What I really want you to take away from my story is that food and nutrition have a huge impact on who you are and what you do. Food influences your mood, your performance, and your ability to act like the supermom you were meant to be.

You simply cannot be the best boss, the best employee, the best mom, the best friend, the best wife, or the best anything without the right fuel for your body. If you are constantly filling it with fast food, diet soda, preservatives, and garbage, you will see the results in what you are able to accomplish. You will see the results in how you feel about yourself.

––––––––––––––––

In this chapter, we will take a good hard look at our health habits. We will look at the foods we are choosing, the way we are moving our bodies, our energy levels and the rest we are taking to recharge.

If you do not have the inside under control, everything outside will be harder. If you are not treating your body like the most important thing you have, nothing else will matter.

FOOD IS EVERYTHING

How many times have you eaten something that you knew would make you feel badly? My best friend in college was lactose intolerant but loved cheese and loved ice cream. (Don't we all.) She knew that if she ate these foods she would feel bloated and have stomach cramps. Most of the time, she avoided the foods. Sometimes, though, it just felt worth it to eat from that delicious cheese tray and worry about the consequences later.

It is so easy to think "just one bite" or "I'll start tomorrow" or "maybe it won't be that bad this time."

It would be easy for me to say to you, "If it makes you feel like crap, don't eat it. Duh. If it gives you brain fog and lethargy and stomach cramps, that food is not for you." Our brains just don't always work that way. The pull of our habits and cravings can be hard to overpower.

> **IF YOU ARE NOT TREATING YOUR BODY LIKE THE MOST IMPORTANT THING YOU HAVE, NOTHING ELSE WILL MATTER.**

So, what can you do? Take one small step. Track your food. That is it. Don't stop eating or drinking anything if you don't want to. Just start tracking it.

You can write it in a notebook. You can use an app on your phone. You can copy the page in your Secrets of Supermom Workbook. You can voice message it into your phone notes. Research has shown that simply tracking what you are eating leads to a change. Maybe you choose a roasted veggie salad instead of a cheesesteak. Maybe you eat three Oreos and not half of the package—or the full package. Maybe you drink more water or less soda.

This one change can lead to bigger changes, better choices, and a greater likelihood of maintaining new food choice habits because you are already in the habit of tracking. Remember how small changes can become big changes from Chapter 1?

If you have low energy, emotional outbursts, overwhelm, limited patience, brain fog, unexplained body pains, headaches, and more, I challenge you to take a look at your food log and see if some of these negative experiences may be alleviated with a change in eating habits.

EXERCISE IS FUN?

I used to hate exercise. I never played sports. I was the worst on any mandated team. I hated running. I hated P.E. class. I hated going to the gym.

My lack of exercise and poor food choices—think 3:00 a.m. burritos—in college caused me to gain about forty pounds. I had really taken that "Freshman Fifteen" and run with it.

Over the years, I tried *a lot* of work out plans. Gym membership, step aerobics, Walk Away the Pounds® on VHS tape, Insanity®, TaeBo®, you name it. I was never consistent, and I never liked it enough to keep going.

Moms would talk about their workouts at dinners out or in the pick-up line. I had nothing to say and was embarrassed by it all. I decided I was just meant to be chubby and uncoordinated.

About three years ago, I won a raffle drawing at the kids' school for a month free of "Frankie's Fitness." Frankie's Fitness was a small group personal training class. Frankie, the owner, taught my class right at our community center. He set up my first class, and he was expecting me. It was three days a week, and the limited class size meant he was waiting on me for every class.

This accountability was exactly what I needed. I didn't miss a single workout that first month. Class was hard, but I signed up and, once again, never looked back.

If I am traveling and have to miss an in-person class, he gives me an alternate workout; I do it in the hotel gym. If I have a meeting and can't make it, I do the workout at home. It is a complete habit for me now, and I never miss it. I even added in more workouts, some walking, and some running, all on my own.

The class created a transformation in me. I am stronger, fitter, and healthier than I have ever been. I feel amazing inside and far more amazing than I ever have outside.

This was not about being skinny—I am not. It wasn't about having six-pack abs and a rock-hard butt—I have neither. It was about finding something I actually liked that I could turn into a habit. It was about finding more energy. It was about feeling strong.

The point of this story is not to shame you into exercise. That clearly never worked for me, and it won't work for you either. My point is that you can move your body in so many ways.

Some people like sports, some like to swim, some like the gym. Some moms do best when they have to sign up for a class or when someone is counting on them to be there, like a neighbor or a friend. A friend of mine pays for a trainer simply because she knows she will never miss a workout when she knows "Maggie with the muscles" is waiting for her.

Find something that works for you. Don't stop trying new things until something clicks.

You must take care of your body; no one else will do it for you. You can't be a supermom if you get exhausted just putting on your super suit.

MOMMY, ARE YOU SLEEPING?

How many times have you gone to bed later than you wanted as a working mom? If you are like most of us, your answer is probably a lot. Maybe you finally made it into bed on time, and the baby woke up just before you drifted off to sleep. Maybe you got involved in a project after the kids finally went to bed and wanted to get "just one more thing" done. Maybe you just got lost in a sea of Netflix shows and social media posts.

Your on-time bedtime quickly went from 9:30 p.m. to 11:45 p.m., and that 5:30 a.m. alarm is going to be…unwelcome.

I used to think that I didn't need to sleep. I would get four or five hours of sleep night after night. I stayed up late working, woke up multiple times to nurse a baby, got up early to start my day, and just kept plowing through life.

I read all the books about how sleep was so important. I just didn't agree with them.

"That's not me," I would think. "I am not like all those other people that need so much sleep."

Then, I started actually exercising regularly. My body needed rest to repair itself from my hard workouts. I didn't need as much sleep earlier in life because I wasn't using my body to its full potential.

Research shows that lack of sleep negatively impacts mood, memory, immune function, and pain sensitivity, increases procrastination, causes weight gain, and makes you more likely to fight with your partner. Whoa.

I don't know about you, but I don't want any of those things in my life. I don't want to be a sad, forgetful, sick, pained, overweight procrastinator that picks fights with my husband. I don't want my hormone balance and brain function to be inhibited.

How can you get more sleep? Turn it all off and get in bed. The obvious step is often hardest.

One way to get more sleep is to schedule your day. If every task has an assigned time, including sleep, you are far more likely to stick to the plan and keep a reasonable bedtime.

Ideally, you will go to bed and wake up at the same time every day. If you want to be a supermom, you need to be disciplined. Going to bed and waking up at different times every day is a sure way to throw off your sleep and your productivity overall.

A few more ways that research says will help with sleep:

- Don't have food, alcohol or caffeine late in the evening
- Make it as dark as possible
- Don't take long naps
- Keep it cool in your room
- Don't exercise late in the day
- Always see your doctor if you are having real trouble going to sleep or staying asleep

---

SUPERMOM SHORTCUT • THE SECRET OF HEALTH • CHAPTER WRAP UP

WHAT WE LEARNED

Nutrition, exercise, and sleep will make or break your ability to be the best in your career and at home. If you do not have the inside under control, everything outside will be harder. This is the *most important* chapter.

HOW WE APPLY IT

- Food: If you know your diet needs small fixes or a complete overhaul, take one small step. Write down everything you eat without changing anything. Ready for something bigger? Give up one food. Drink one more cup of water a day. Drink one less Diet Dr. Pepper. Once you have your small win, think about a larger diet change to start to examine your habits around food and determine what foods make you a powerhouse and what foods make you a blob.

- Exercise: You must move your body every day. Hate to exercise? Keep trying new things until you find something that sticks or find an accountability partner.
- Sleep: If you are eating right and exercising, you need sleep to rest and repair your body. The best way to get more sleep is to schedule it. Set your go-to-sleep and wake-up times and stick to them.

ONE SMALL STEP

Decide today what one thing you will do to improve your health and write it in your workbook or on a simple sheet of paper or post-it note. Then look at it every morning. Decide each day that you will be consistent with your one small step.

WHAT COMES NEXT

In the next chapter, we will dive deep into attitude. A healthy body does no good if your mind is stuck in a negative feedback loop. A healthy body and a healthy mind are essential for any high-performing mom.

CHAPTER 6
SUPERMOMS CAN MAKE ANYTHING FUN

THE SECRET OF ATTITUDE

> "I know it is wet and the sun is not sunny, but we can have lots of good fun that is funny."
>
> — Dr. Seuss, *The Cat in the Hat*[20]

> "Attitude is a choice. Happiness is a choice. Optimism is a choice. Kindness is a choice. Giving is a choice. Respect is a choice. Whatever choice you make makes you. Choose wisely."
>
> — Roy T. Bennett, *The Light in the Heart*[21]

The clients filed into the conference room one by one. Some had traveled in late and already looked tired. Some were happy and ready to start our week-long round of meetings. We called it a "camp," but it was essentially a week of intense meetings in order to get as much done as possible with all the key players in the room.

Working for a large corporation with many clients, we are often not in the same office or the same city as our teams. This type of meeting was our opportunity to build the team and build the infrastructure of our project.

The camps were grueling. Long hours followed by long dinners. Early mornings. A giant list of tasks and project plans to complete. The meetings were certainly necessary but not always what we would call fun.

Plenty of Fortune 500 companies have strategies to make meetings like this fun. Icebreakers, snacks, team-building activities, breaks to socialize, you name it.

We used a bell.

In the middle of the table sat a bell. The bell looked like any bell you might see on a teacher's desk or at a hotel check-in. It sat right in the center of the long conference table.

Anytime a team completed one of their tasks, and it was considered 100% done, they could ring the bell.

You might be thinking to yourself, "Why would anyone care about ringing a dumb old bell?" I am telling you, try it at your next meeting. Try it out at home. Tell your kids that as soon as they clean their room, they get to ring the bell. You will see the power of the bell.

Close your eyes and picture yourself in a casino. What do you hear? Lots and lots of bells, right?

Let's talk about what is happening here. Why would ringing a bell change anything? The bell changed the attitude about the meeting. When someone would ding-ding-ding that bell, everyone would laugh or cheer. Even the most stoic of attendees would at least smile. Sometimes that's all you can hope for.

Instead of feeling like a never-ending sea of tasks, every time the bell would ring, the team felt closer to the overall goal.

We were getting there. We were making things happen.

It also gave a reward for getting a task done. Instead of feeling, "Ugh...I have to write a 25-page standard operating procedure," team members thought, "As soon as I get my 25-page standard operating procedure done, I get to ring the bell and my tasks are complete!"

Do you see the difference? Do you see how the task is the same but the thoughts are different? The *attitude* is different.

Finally, it encouraged healthy competition between teams to get done first. It was like a game. You certainly didn't want to be the only one that *didn't* get to ring the bell. Think about how fast your kids could clean their room if there was a competition for who could get done first.

―――――――――――

If you ask me, attitude is *everything*. In a brilliant study done at Stanford, researchers found that kids who had a positive attitude about math actually performed better. In addition, they found that students with a positive attitude had better brain function, memory, and problem-solving ability while doing math problems than even their peers with higher IQs.[22]

Your attitude about something will help you do it better. Better even than someone who is smarter than you. Win.

Your team will achieve goals better than other teams if they have a better attitude. Your kids will do better in school, complete their chores better, and be better at sports if they have a positive attitude. You will do better at everything if you choose to see the positive in the experience.

Every day, we have to do things we want to do and things we don't want to do. All of us. You choose your attitude about the task. Take simply getting up in the morning, for example.

How do you feel when your alarm goes off or when you first wake up in the morning? Are you excited about the day? Or are you more likely to be angry, irritated, and pulling the covers back over your head?

I love mornings. I love to wake up early and get things done. I love my morning routine that I described in the first part of this book. I love to get the day going when it is still dark and experience sunrise. I have had this attitude about mornings for as long as I can remember.

I think it started with waking up as a child. My dad would open the door to my room and say, "Good morning, Mary Sunshine!" or "Up and at 'em, Adam Ant!" He would drink coffee and sing through his morning routine of shower and shave. He was obviously a morning person.

I want to cultivate that same attitude starting the day in my own home with my own children. They all still wake up early and, so far, are always in a good mood. To be fair, none of them are teenagers yet, so I think all bets are off when we reach that stage. Maybe I will need to write another book.

When they are not awake or when we have to wake them early, we sing *"The Good Morning Song."* It goes like this:

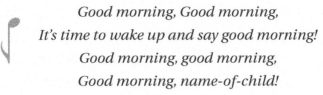

Good morning, Good morning,
It's time to wake up and say good morning!
Good morning, good morning,
Good morning, name-of-child!

As they get older, the kids have learned to sing this to each other. One recent morning, Kaden told me that he woke up the girls, knowing that it was getting close to school time.

I said to him, "You woke them up?"

He said, "Yes. Don't worry. I sang them the good morning song."

"Good boy!"

We cultivate a positive attitude in other ways at home. It is not about big things. It is specifically about small attitude changes.

Each night at dinner, we do "best/worst." Each family member goes around the table and tells the best of their day and the worst of their day. If another child is sleeping over with us or someone comes over for dinner, they get to participate in "best/worst" too.

Do we eat dinner together every night? Unless a parent is on a business trip or a child is at a sleepover, yes, we sit down together for dinner every night. Years ago, I read an article that detailed how research showed that families who ate dinner together were stronger, had a lower likelihood of drug use in adolescence, were better at communication, and were happier overall. I can't find that research for the life of me, but I sure took its lesson to heart. If all it took was dinner together, I was in.

Every night, we sit down for dinner together and a different person goes first. Each family member is expected to tell the very best thing that happened to them that day and the worst thing that happened. It gives every family member a chance to share their wins of the day and their struggles. It also forces them to find something positive about the day, even if it was a rough one.

Even the tiniest ones participate in this tradition. We started it about four years ago when Kami was only three years old and Kellen was still on the inside. Her "best/worst" was the same every day—best was "eating this dinner" and worst was "I not got a worst"—but she still participated and eventually figured it out.

Attitude can so often be tied to gratitude. This tradition challenges the family to think about something they are grateful for about their day and name it the best of the day. For the month of November, we shift our "best/worst" to "thankful/grateful" where they share something they are grateful for as part of celebration the U.S. holiday of Thanksgiving.

Attitude has been linked with improved stress management, better immunity, increased resilience, and lower levels of depression.[23]

A positive attitude is not the same as unrealistic optimism. It is not being naïve or impractical. In a study conducted in 1980, Dr. Neil Weinstein found that students with unrealistic optimism had a tendency to believe they were invulnerable or at a very low risk of suffering, illness, misfortune, and becoming a victim.

This was even in the presence of data that showed the opposite to be true.[24]

A positive attitude is instead deciding to look for the good in a situation, the benefit, the possibility of hope versus dwelling on the bad. A positive attitude does not ignore risks or costs or the potential of negative outcomes. It doesn't pretend that something is not hard. It is instead a way of thinking that allows for a positive approach to life and to the problems within.

> A POSITIVE ATTITUDE DOES NOT IGNORE RISKS OR COSTS OR THE POTENTIAL OF NEGATIVE OUTCOMES. IT DOESN'T PRETEND THAT SOMETHING IS NOT HARD. IT IS INSTEAD A WAY OF THINKING THAT ALLOWS FOR A POSITIVE APPROACH TO LIFE AND TO THE PROBLEMS WITHIN.

How can you encourage a positive attitude…

…in yourself?

- Start a gratitude practice. Mine is very simple. Every morning, I think about one thing I am grateful for from the day before. Simple and effective.
- Before you take on a hard challenge, think about how you will feel at the end. Visualize how you will go through the challenge and complete it well. Before I present to my executive management team, for example, I think about how proud I will feel when I can present clearly, be concise, and answer all of their questions.

- Remember that you are the only one that controls your attitude. Others can act any way they want, but only you control the way you think and feel about it.
- Steer clear of Negative Nellies. If you have a hard time encouraging a positive attitude in yourself, definitely spend as little time as possible with friends or co-workers who tend to be negative. They may drag you down with them. I call this the "culture of complaint," and we discuss this more in Chapter 15.
- Curb negative self-talk. Saying things like "I can't do it," "I am not smart enough," "It's just impossible," or "This will definitely go horribly" is a sure way to make you believe those statements to be true.

…in your home?

- Everyone has to clean house or at least clean up. Blast music, put on costumes, ring bells! I have a girlfriend from one of my first jobs that used to play music and put on crazy hats when she would clean the house. Y'all, she lived alone! It felt like fun dress-up-time instead of boring house cleaning. Now that she has three kids, they all wear hats, and the house stays gloriously organized.
- Ask your children about the best part of their day. Not only does this encourage positive attitudes and gratitude but it also gets the communication flowing!

- Tell your partner why you are excited to take on a challenge, like cleaning out the garage, and how happy you will feel when it is perfect and organized.

…in your career or business?

- Complete a "post-hoc" with your team after a big presentation. Ask them about the things that went really well and the things they feel they can improve for next time. An honest review helps your team to feel positively about the successes and initiate positive momentum toward improvement for anything that didn't go well.
- Before a sales call, think about how you will succeed and provide value to your client. Get yourself pumped for that call!
- Your manager just gave you a big project, and it is harder than you expected. Think about how much you will learn in the process, how you will make connections with other departments to help it go well, and how you will build a positive communication pathway with your manager.

SUPERMOM SHORTCUT • THE SECRET OF ATTITUDE • CHAPTER WRAP UP

WHAT WE LEARNED

A positive attitude is linked with improved performance, better immunity, lower levels of depression, increased resilience, and better stress management. When we cultivate a positive attitude in our teams, our homes, and ourselves, we give ourselves the chance to be better at the tasks we perform, feel happier about them, and be healthier overall.

HOW WE APPLY IT

In order to start your positive attitude within, begin with the following steps:

- Start a gratitude practice.
- Before you take on a hard challenge, visualize how you will feel at the end.
- Remember that you are the only one who controls your attitude.
- Avoid Negative Nellies.
- Curb negative self-talk.

ONE SMALL STEP

Start a gratitude practice, and do it every day. When you have your habit in place, add in your family, and build on from there.

WHAT COMES NEXT

Sometimes being a supermom is just plain hard. You will encounter hard things and have to develop methods for building strength and courage within yourself. In the next chapter, we discuss the secret of strength.

CHAPTER 7
SUPERMOMS DO HARD THINGS

THE SECRET OF STRENGTH

"That's the hard thing about hard things—there is no formula
for dealing with them."
— Ben Horowitz, *The Hard Thing About Hard Things*[25]

"In the midst of winter, I found there was, within
me, an invincible summer."
— Albert Camus, *Retour to Tipasa*[26]

I had just boarded the flight and felt a twinge of pain. Just weeks
before, I went in for outpatient surgery to remove the "evidence
of pregnancy" from my presumed miscarriage. The cramps were
long gone at this point. The twinge was unexpected.

This was my first pregnancy. Jeremy and I had been married
less than a year and started trying to get pregnant almost immediately. Nearing thirty and wanting multiple children, we knew
now was the time and the time was now.

After months and months of trying, I was over the moon to see that positive "pregnant" on my way-too-expensive digital pregnancy tests. I didn't want to just see two pink lines. I wanted to see the word PREGNANT clear as day. So, I splurged. I bought *a lot* of those tests.

We found the most wonderful OB/GYN. I was excited for my appointment and could not wait for that first ultrasound. It did not go as planned. Despite the positive test, there was no baby. No heartbeat.

We scheduled my appointment, I had the surgery, and then I went right back to work and travel. Work was a good distraction for me and kept me moving forward.

So, there I was aboard my flight to Philadelphia.

My hCG levels, the hormone they test to indicate pregnancy, had remained elevated, and I knew there was technically a possibility I actually had an ectopic pregnancy instead of a miscarriage. An ectopic pregnancy meant that an egg was fertilized and implanted somewhere outside my uterus. It was unlikely, but there was a small possibility. If it were true, it would be an emergency.

As we took off from Sky Harbor International Airport in Phoenix, I felt another twinge, a pretty sharp pain this time, in my lower abdomen. The trip would only be a few days. I was sure the pain would subside.

We landed in Philadelphia, I picked up a rental car, and I drove as fast as I could to my hotel. The pain continued to get worse.

It was after midnight, and I was exhausted, but I could barely sleep. I tossed and turned trying to get into a comfortable position. I finally curled into a ball, alone in the hotel bed. In the early morning hours, I put on clothes and headed to the hospital. I should have been working there in just a few hours and would instead become a patient.

I told the nurses my symptoms, remembered every hCG level that had been drawn by heart, and told them I was worried it was an ectopic pregnancy. After several exams and a quick ultrasound, we confirmed my fear. My left fallopian tube had a mass. It was not salvageable. They would need to remove it immediately and would try to save my ovary.

They were taking my tube, a body part quite necessary to make babies. And I wanted lots of babies. And I was all alone.

The surgery was successful, they saved the ovary, and they admitted me to stay overnight, fearful of sending me back to the hotel. I was all alone, but everyone was incredibly caring. The next morning, they released me, and I drove myself back to my hotel. I packed, drove myself to the airport, navigated security in a wheelchair, and flew back home. It was hard. It was scary, and I was alone.

You already know that the overall ending was happy. My single tube and I, with necessary help from my husband, went on to successfully bear four babies that made it out healthy and happy. Two girls and two boys.

My kids and I talk about that baby that could have been. We talk about how life would be different if Kinley wasn't the oldest and bossiest. We talk about how, if I had stopped at four kids, we wouldn't have Kellen. They decided baby number one was a boy since we have a girl-boy-girl-boy pattern. We talk about how that Hulk baby—the one that busted through the tube—was never meant to be.

———————————

Every day we encounter hard things. We endure hard parts of life and hard parts of parenting. We encounter loss and grief. We have to make hard choices.

As supermoms, with so many balls in the air, how do we come through hard things stronger and with more grit and determination than ever before? How do we thrive in the midst of hard things instead of just barely survive?

We will never be successful if we cannot navigate hard things. We simply cannot be the supermom we were meant to be if we avoid the hard. Trying to become a parent is hard. Being a parent is hard. Climbing the career ladder is hard. Building a business is hard.

All hard things are fraught with reward. You have to learn how to endure them, to navigate them well, to make it through stronger. You have to learn to make the journey count.

YOU HAVE TO LEARN TO MAKE THE JOURNEY COUNT.

If you think about it, you are probably already doing so many hard things.

- Getting a master's degree while chasing around two toddlers
- Working on a promotion while caring for a newborn
- Traveling cross-country and presenting at conferences while very pregnant
- Breastfeeding for a year even though you went back to work after eight weeks
- Starting a business with three babies under three at home
- Dealing with miscarriage while serving your clients well

In this book, we will talk about a number of strategies that high-performing supermoms use to do all sorts of hard things. Let's talk about some basic steps for any challenge.

1.	ACKNOWLEDGE THAT THE SITUATION OR CHOICE IS HARD.
2.	ACCEPT THAT YOU MAY FEEL STRESSED, OVERWHELMED, OR EMOTIONALLY DRAINED.
3.	REALIZE YOUR THOUGHTS.
4.	UNDERSTAND THAT THIS IS YOUR HARD THING AND NO ONE ELSE'S. YOU DO YOU.
5.	FIND SUPPORT.
6.	PRIORITIZE PHYSICAL WELLNESS.
7.	FIND JOY.
8.	BREAK IT DOWN.
9.	TAKE THE FIRST STEP.
10.	CELEBRATE YOUR WINS (EVEN THE SMALL ONES)!

ACKNOWLEDGE THAT THE SITUATION OR CHOICE IS HARD.

It is almost impossible to demonstrate the courage to do something hard without acknowledging that the thing just might suck. It might not be fun. It might be scary.

It is okay to say it is going to be hard.

The acknowledgement that the decision will not be an easy one is the first step in deciding to do it anyway. It is the first step in making a plan to actually make it to the finish line.

When I was at the hospital, alone, I thought, "Wow, this sucks! This might be one of the hardest things I have done in my young life." I didn't sugar coat the situation.

In my particular story, I didn't choose the hard thing. The ectopic pregnancy was not my fault, and I had no way of knowing what would happen. It didn't change the fact that it was a hard thing I needed to navigate to be stronger and get what I ultimately wanted in the end.

Maybe you have a loss to navigate too. Or maybe your hard thing is fully "self-inflicted." Did you decide to start a master's program when your baby was only a month old? Did you decide to start a business with four small kids at home?

The steps are the same. Supermoms—those of us that want to perform at the highest levels and have joy and fervor unlike anyone else—have to take the same path when things get hard. It doesn't matter if you chose your hard or if your hard chose you.

ACCEPT THAT YOU MAY FEEL STRESSED, OVERWHELMED, OR EMOTIONALLY DRAINED.

When we decide to move forward into a hard thing, we know it will be hard. Sure, working full time and building a business while pregnant with twins will be hard. Duh. What we fail to often think about are the emotions that may strike at any point in the process.

By failing to identify the emotions, we fail to plan for them. By failing to plan for them, we don't have a strategy to work through the pain. Not only do we want to identify what emotions might come up, but what will we do if that happens. We need a *plan*.

If we identify the plan before the emotion hits, we are much more likely to actually be able to manage it. If we don't manage it, it can derail us at best and stop us completely at worst.

What was my plan when in the hospital? *If I feel scared, I will talk to my nurse.* The nurses felt horrible that I was alone and treated me with a wonderful warmth. *If I feel overwhelmed, I will write down my feelings about this baby who was not meant to be.*

Here are some other examples:

- When I feel overwhelmed, I will stop and focus only on my breathing for ten minutes.
- When I feel stressed, I will focus only on the feelings in my body.
- When I feel like I am going to cry, I will call my mom, and I will cry long and loud.

REALIZE YOUR THOUGHTS.

Our thoughts control our feelings and our actions. When we allow ourselves to simply react or have an emotion without actually understanding the thought behind it, we start to feel out of control. We start to think that our brain has a mind of its own and that we are just on a wild ride.

Instead, I want you to think about the thoughts you are having around your hard thing, the thoughts that are triggering the emotions we talked about in the previous step. The goal is not to judge the thoughts or to decide whether they are negative or positive. The goal is simply to identify them.

For example, my thoughts during my stay in the hospital looked something like this:

After this, I will never be able to have a baby.

I know I have a good doctor with a good team.

What if surgery goes wrong?

My husband will think this is my fault.

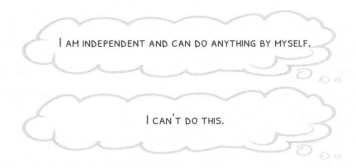

Were these thoughts all rational? Definitely not. Were they all positive or negative? Also, no.

The goal is to identify the thoughts, determine the emotion they are causing, and decide if that thought is worth keeping. Identifying the thoughts that are feeding your emotions allows you to change those thoughts. It also allows you to keep the thought if it somehow serves you.

Without understanding the thoughts in your brain and only feeling the overwhelming emotions, you really will feel out of control.

UNDERSTAND THAT THIS IS YOUR HARD THING AND NO ONE ELSE'S. YOU DO YOU.

You get to choose how you do your hard thing. This isn't about how your mom would do it or your best friend would do it or how your partner thinks you should do it.

Stay in your lane, put on your blinders, and remember that you are the only one that will come out on the other side. If this seems like a tall ask for you, go back to Chapter 2 on confidence and people-pleasing.

"Maybe you should get a second opinion?"

"Are you sure that Jeremy shouldn't come to be with you?"

Family and friends certainly had opinions on what I should do to get through my hard thing. Ultimately, it was my decision. If I let other people's opinions get in my way, I may not have made the best decision for me.

By getting through the first three steps, you will know your thoughts and your feelings. You will be able to make the best decision. You do you.

FIND SUPPORT.

It might seem odd to tell you that you need people when I just told you to put on your blinders. You need others that you can rely on to help you through the rough patches and cheer with you when you make strides forward (see "Celebrate your wins!" below).

This might not be your partner, spouse, or sister. Those closest to us know us really well, but they aren't always our biggest supporters. In order to really move forward well, you want someone who supports you but is also willing to challenge your thoughts.

You might find this in a friend. You might also find this in a counselor, therapist, or coach. The goal is that you do not feel alone in your journey.

PRIORITIZE PHYSICAL WELLNESS.

Earlier in this book we talked about the importance of physical wellness and included large and small things you can do to feel strong, smart, and healthy. Research shows the highest performers are also the healthiest.

They exercise more and often have a specific exercise regimen. They eat better and choose foods wisely. They know the impact of sleep and rest. They manage stress in order to better cope with the unexpected.

If you can do nothing but prioritize the health of your body, you will see that *everything* comes easier. Hard things are not quite as hard when you have a healthy body and mind.

FIND JOY.

In all things, a positive can be found. I firmly believe that a silver lining can be found in nearly every situation, nearly every hard thing.

Think about the last hard thing you did or hard experience you went through. Can you find a positive?

As I talked to my surgeon following surgery, he mentioned how lucky I was that my tube had not ruptured. I was lucky to have come to the hospital when I did, lucky that they were able to save my ovary, despite losing the tube. It truly could have been worse.

Sometimes you can find true joy in your hard thing. A success. A baby step forward. A chance to learn a new skill, beat a challenge, or meet a new person. Sometimes the joy is found in the fact that the situation could have been so much worse.

Finding joy can look a lot like gratitude. We talked more about gratitude in Chapter 3 including how you can work it into your every day.

BREAK IT DOWN.

Your hard thing cannot be accomplished in a single action. If it could, it wouldn't be hard. The best way to do a really hard thing is to break it down into the smallest steps.

Start at the end of the journey. Steven Covey, in his book *The Seven Habits of Highly Effective People*, calls this beginning with the end in mind[27]. Think about how life will look when you are through the hard thing.

Is it that you will have a degree in hand? Will you have the raise or the promotion? Will you be at peace with your stage of grief? Start there.

Then, work backwards. How long will it take to get to the end goal and what are the steps to get there? Write them down. This is a great place to use your Secrets of Supermom Workbook.

For me, when sitting in that hospital bed and getting ready for surgery, my end goal was to be home and feel pain free. My steps:

1. Use "anxiety breathing"—we will talk more about anxiety breathing in Chapter 10—to calmly prepare for surgery.

2. Talk to my mom.

3. Undergo surgery.

4. Stay overnight, listen to the nurses, and be discharged in the morning as planned.

5. Go to the hotel, pack, and drive to the airport.

6. Check my bag and request medical transport to prevent walking all the way to my gate.

7. Fly home.

8. Have Jeremy pick me up from the airport.

9. Rest and follow the doctor's instructions.

It may seem silly to break a traumatic event into steps to recovery. It might be easier for some to see this concept in completing a hard thing like starting a business, building a website, or writing a book.

Here is what I think. Hard things, any hard thing, can be scary and traumatic and emotional. Breaking any hard thing into small steps makes it seem manageable, doable. To think about going through surgery, driving myself around Philadelphia, and making it home all on my own was overwhelming.

Instead, looking at it one step at a time made me feel like I could handle it. I could do this. And you can do this too! Any hard thing!

TAKE THE FIRST STEP.

Just start. The first step of your journey is always the hardest one, so just get in motion. If the task or the journey is exceptionally hard or long, start small. Since taking the first step is the hardest, getting yourself in motion by choosing something small makes you more likely to take step two, three, and forty-seven.

My first step was simply to breathe. To relax and calm myself. I wanted to feel ready for the surgery I was about to undertake, not anxious and not like the basket case right under the surface.

CELEBRATE YOUR WINS (EVEN THE SMALL ONES)!

It is time to celebrate! Remember that you deserve to enjoy your successes. Supermoms know that they can't maintain continued effort without finding the joy in the journey.

Find a key milestone in your process and schedule a celebration. Yes, I said schedule it. Make it a step in your process if you need to do that, but make it happen. For example:

1. Write Chapter One
2. Write Chapter Two
3. Write Chapter Three
4. Celebrate with a pedicure!
5. Write Chapter Four

It is impossible to do hard things without taking a moment to realize your wins. It is impossible to continue to maintain a necessary level of drive and perseverance if you don't recognize how amazing you actually are for doing hard things!

———————

SUPERMOM SHORTCUT • THE SECRET OF STRENGTH • CHAPTER WRAP UP

WHAT WE LEARNED

Life is fraught with hard choices and hard situations. Sometimes we choose to do something hard, like getting a master's degree while parenting two toddlers and working full time. Sometimes hard things are not our choice like a miscarriage or loss of a parent. The better we are at navigating hard things, the better we will be at leading happy and productive lives.

HOW WE APPLY IT

Ten key steps to doing hard things:

1. Acknowledge that the situation or choice is hard.
2. Accept that you may feel stressed, overwhelmed, or emotionally drained.
3. Realize your thoughts.
4. Understand that this is your hard thing and no one else's. You do you.
5. Find support.
6. Prioritize physical wellness.
7. Find joy.
8. Break it down.
9. Take the first step.
10. Celebrate your wins!

ONE SMALL STEP

The first step to doing hard things is simply acknowledging that the situation or choice is hard and that you will do it anyway. You will take the first step with courage because the only way forward is through.

Write down your hard thing in your workbook or on a piece of paper and look at it every day. When you are ready to conquer all the steps, walk through the full chapter.

WHAT COMES NEXT

In the next chapter, we will talk about one of the biggest things that separates busy moms from supermoms: happiness. The secret of supermoms is they are busy, successful, and *happy* at the same time.

CHAPTER 8
SUPERMOMS SEEK JOY

THE SECRET OF HAPPINESS

"Too many people measure how successful they are by how much money they make or the people that they associate with. In my opinion, true success should be measured by how happy you are."

— Richard Branson[28]

"If you want to be happy, do not dwell in the past, do not worry about the future, focus on living fully in the present."

— Roy T. Bennett, *The Light in the Heart*[29]

I secretly believed I was lucky.

I had never told anyone, but I still thought it often. I would get great parking spots. I won the raffle at my daughter's theatre performance. I won a Batman car seat at a Meet-A-Superhero event. My kids went crazy over it!

I thought I was lucky despite having an ectopic pregnancy and losing not only the baby but one of my fallopian tubes before I ever had children. I thought I was lucky despite being diagnosed with melanoma at 34 years old and now wearing a three-and-a-half-inch scar across my chest. I thought I was lucky despite parents that divorced after almost 33 years of marriage. I thought I was lucky despite a multitude of daily challenges. How could I possibly feel lucky?

A few years ago, I got a text message from a friend. It said, "I've come to realize that easy street is just not the path set for me and challenges are around every corner. Just have to keep fighting."

This was a lightbulb moment for me.

I believed I was lucky because I *chose* to believe I was lucky. I chose to be happy and feel lucky and have a positive attitude. I decided to focus on the things that brought me joy, brought me *luck*, instead of the unhappy. I had decided years before that I would not be defined by adversity; I would learn and continue to move from a place of optimism.

Being happy is a choice.

You can live in a pity party of sadness. You can focus on every bad thing that happens to you every day and let it destroy your mood, your attitude, and your joy. Or you can choose to be happy.

Before we talk about ways to focus on happiness and what you can do to be happier in life, I want to throw in a caveat. When I say happiness is a choice, I am not talking about moms suffering from mental

BEING HAPPY IS A CHOICE.

health disorders. I am not telling those of you struggling with Major Depressive Disorder that you are choosing to be sad. I am not telling those of you dealing with Bipolar Disorder that you should just be happy.

Solid mental health is critical to function in life in general, and certainly critical for the mom who is juggling a career and a family. If that is you, this is not your chapter. Your first focus must be to stabilize your mental health with the help of a medical and/or mental health professional.

———————

Research shows that happiness has a multitude of benefits. You know it feels good to be happy. Here are some other reasons to engage in happiness practices:

- Happy people make more money.
- Happy people have better immunity and live longer.
- Happy people are more productive at work.
- Happy people manage stress better.
- Happy people have better relationships.
- Happy people can see the big picture with more clarity.
- Happy people have healthier lifestyles.
- Happy people feel more control over their lives.

There are specific, tangible things you can do to bring more joy to your life and to focus on happiness. If you are struggling to be happy, any one of these can be used to allow a greater focus on enjoyment of life.

THE HAPPINESS LIST

Make a happiness list. Get out a sheet of paper or your Secrets of Supermom Workbook and make a list of all the things that make you happy. This is *your* list. Don't write things that *should* make you happy. Write only things that *actually* make you happy. If your friend loves running, but you hate it, don't put it on the list.

My list might look something like this:

- Singing at the top of my lungs to music blaring in my car
- Reading a hard-copy book
- Cuddling with Juno, our Great Dane
- Watching Kinley perform on stage
- Looking at photo albums
- Taking a bike ride with the kids
- Listening to a podcast about goal setting
- Eating slowly at a restaurant (generally this means the kids can't be there...they are not ready for the long, relaxing dinner just yet)
- Seeing a movie and eating buttered popcorn
- A long hug
- Hearing Kellen yell "It's snuggle time!" and running to snuggle in my lap with his eyes closed
- Dinner with my best friend

Once you have your list, keep it in a place where you can refer to it often. The goal is to incorporate something from the list into your life every day, if even for just five minutes.

Deciding to do something that makes you happy, every single day, is a wonderfully effective way to maintain a greater level of overall happiness.

LEARN SOMETHING NEW

In *The Happiness Project,*[30] Gretchen Rubin refers to an "atmosphere of growth." She says, based on research, if you are not growing, learning, and experiencing new things, you are more likely to be unhappy or feel stuck in your life.

How can you apply this in your own life? Sign up for a class to learn something new. Join a book club and read new books. Volunteer for a project at work that you have not done in the past. Listen to a podcast on a new topic.

The key in this path to happy is to enjoy the journey. The happiness doesn't come from learning the new thing. The joy isn't knowing how to make French pastries at the end of your culinary class. It is in the learning. It is in the small improvements you make as you continue to learn. Don't forget to enjoy the ride or the destination won't be nearly as sweet—except in the case of French pastries, I suppose.

GET BETTER AND STRONGER

In the same vein as learning something new, we feel happy when we get better and stronger. When we feel like we are improving in some way, we have an increase of dopamine in our brain that says, "Yes, keep doing that. You are getting better!"

This doesn't necessarily mean physically stronger. It could mean lifting more weight at the gym. It could also mean becoming a stronger writer, a stronger speaker, a stronger decorator, or a stronger organizer.

FOCUS ON RELATIONSHIPS

We are humans, and humans need humans. Nurturing your relationships is critical to ultimate happiness as well as longevity and satisfaction with life.

Who are the most important people in your life? Your partner, your children, your parents, best friend, favorite neighbor? If you look at your last week, can you find ways that you focused on relationships with these people?

If not, it is time to prioritize those relationships. It is important to remember that this is not about quantity of time but about quality of time. Sitting on the couch next to your husband for an hour every night and watching Netflix will not give you the same connection as a focused date night once a week.

My best friend and I don't have time to actually talk very often because life is just crazy. Instead, we send each other long voice texts. We get to stay connected with limited time, and it still sort of feels like talking.

Protect your important relationships, and don't let task lists and activities get in the way of the people that matter most.

BE A HELPING HAND

People like to help people. Research has shown over and again that altruism, helping other people without an expectation of "payback," increases feelings of happiness.

When I was in high school, I volunteered for a teen suicide hotline. I answered calls to help other teens through hard situations and help them access resources in the community. I loved this role, and it led me on lifelong volunteer path.

You don't have to be a formal volunteer. There are daily opportunities to help someone else. You can certainly volunteer—the world needs it, trust me—but helping does not have to be formalized. You can hold a door for someone, pick up someone's dropped keys in the grocery store, or send treats for a class party at your kid's school.

SHOW APPRECIATION

We went deeper into the importance of gratitude for our attitude toward life, happiness, and the importance of a daily gratitude practice in previous chapters.

Appreciation is the expression of that gratitude. Although the internal feeling of gratitude is beneficial to mental health, the outward expression can increase that benefit.

Write personal thank-you notes. Give hugs. Say thank you. Give compliments. Send a text message. Do you love someone's dress at the bank? Tell them. Did you think about your girlfriend from high school today and how much you appreciated her deep chats? Reach out and tell her. Did your kiddo bring you a flower unexpectedly? Say thanks, and give a big, long hug.

HUGS

Speaking of hugs, did you know that a twenty-second hug can improve your health, lower your stress levels, and increase happiness? Research on hugs shows that a twenty-second hug can increase oxytocin (the love hormone), reduce heart rate in stressful situations, and reduce blood pressure.[31]

Get more hugs, and give more hugs.

THE MIRACLE OF FORGIVENESS

Are you holding a grudge? Is there someone you can't seem to forgive?

Forgiveness is critical to lifetime happiness. Many people think that forgiveness is saying "it's okay" to someone that has wronged or victimized you. In reality, forgiveness has nothing to do with the other person at all.

Forgiveness is the act of releasing your own anger, resentment, or grudge. It is freeing yourself from these feelings that will ultimately weigh you down, increase cortisol levels, and contribute to declines in mental health.

Forgiveness doesn't only mean forgiving others. It means forgiving yourself too. Are you holding a grudge against yourself that is limiting your confidence and your happiness? It's time to let that go.

SET BOUNDARIES

Happy people say no. Plain and simple. In order for you to be as happy as possible, you will have to be able to set boundaries. When you feel taken advantage of, you feel the opposite of happy.

This one is especially hard for me. I really like to say yes. If I can make something happen, I like to say yes. Do we have time to get from baseball practice, to the birthday party, and back to the football game? Then, it's a yes! Can I make cupcakes for the bake sale between dance rehearsals? Then, it's a yes! Can I squeeze in an extra two-hour business teleconference a week to be part of a new initiative? Then, it's a yes!

Sometimes, though, that means that my schedule is just so full that there is room for nothing else. If a really amazing opportunity presents itself, your schedule should not be so full with "yeses" that you have to say no to the big goal, the one that could boost success and happiness at the same time.

Your schedule should not be so full that you are only busy and not happy. Busy is not a badge of honor, but a smile definitely is.

THE HAPPINESS MINDSET

Remember I told you how I believed I was lucky? That belief allowed me to consistently look for things that proved I was lucky. Why?

There is a phenomenon called confirmation bias. Essentially, this bias says that we look for information to favor our current beliefs. My belief that I was lucky caused me to look for things that *proved* I was lucky. Instead of focusing on examples where I was certainly *not* lucky, like the pregnancy loss or the cancer, I focused on the luck.

You can do the same by deciding that you are a happy person. I am a happy person, thus I will look for ways to prove that I am happy.

You might have a day filled with stressors, traffic, and yelling kids. The person that knows they are a happy person remembers to delight in the small things and can put the other stresses of life aside.

SUPERMOM SHORTCUT • THE SECRET OF HAPPINESS • CHAPTER WRAP UP

WHAT WE LEARNED

The ultimate goal of life is happiness. Happy people experience better mood, better health, and a better life than those who are unhappy. To be a supermom, you must be happy. There is no point in winning all the career awards and being a high-performing mom if you are miserable.

HOW WE APPLY IT

Sometimes happiness feels like it just comes to us. Other times, it is a struggle. Here are some ways to make sure to prioritize happiness and even to cultivate it:

- The Happiness List: Make a list of everything that makes you happy and work at least one thing into each day.
- Learn Something New: Learning a new concept promotes a growth mindset and increases joy.
- Get Better and Stronger: Working on something? Continue to get better, stronger, and enjoy that journey to be happy.

- Focus on Relationships: Your people are the most important thing in your life. Prioritize them.
- Be a Helping Hand: Helping other people, without expecting anything in return, is a great way to boost your mood.
- Show Appreciation: Feeling grateful? Tell someone, show someone, love on someone.
- Hugs: A twenty-second hug can do wonders for your mood, and theirs.
- The Miracle of Forgiveness: If you are holding a grudge, it is influencing your ability to be completely happy. Forgive others and forgive yourself.
- Set Boundaries: Setting boundaries allows you to say yes to the right things and cultivate the best life.
- The Happiness Mindset: Decide you are a happy person, and you will automatically look for ways to prove it.

ONE SMALL STEP

Write down your happiness list and decide that you will focus on including one thing every day that makes you wonderfully happy.

WHAT COMES NEXT

In the next chapter, we will explore motivation and energy. A supermom has to find ways to motivate herself to go, go, go, even when she doesn't feel like it.

CHAPTER 9
SUPERMOMS CAN GO, GO, GO

THE SECRET OF MOTIVATION

Many people, they've gone weeks without being motivated. They're going through the emotions but there's no energy. There's no emotional pull towards something better. And because they're lacking that emotional pull, what ends up happening? They dog it, they don't contribute as much. They react and sort of create and all of a sudden a couple weeks later, they're like, I don't know why I'm so unfulfilled. Well, no doubt you're so unfulfilled because you haven't been tapping into that emotion of motivation. **When we lack motivation, it is a slippery slope to suffering.**

— Brendan Burchard, *The Brendan Show Podcast*[32]

A man doesn't need brilliance or genius, all he needs is energy.

— Albert M. Greenfield

"I just didn't feel like doing anything today."
"I just couldn't motivate myself to get going."

"I have such a hard time staying motivated at work. I just want to be home with the kids."

"I don't have motivation to put forth any extra effort."

"I can't stay driven."

"After such a long day, it is hard to be motivated to be "on" for my family."

Do you ever just wake up and not want to do *anything*? Moms I surveyed for this book struggled with motivation, drive, and the energy to keep pushing forward.

I often get the question, "Are you always this energetic?" or "Do you ever get tired?" Sometimes I don't think these questions are necessarily meant as compliments. Regardless, I have taught myself to be high energy and to be consistently able to find motivation from within myself.

Staying motivated can be tough even when things are easy. It is a compounded struggle when things are hard, when you are super busy, or when stress is high.

Do you struggle with motivation? Do you find it hard to get going sometimes, even when you know you are on a deadline? Do you find yourself constantly pushing yourself out of a "rut"? This chapter is for you!

———————————

Think about that internal drive that makes you want more—to be more, to have more, to make a difference. The drive is coming from inside you and nowhere else. No one is telling you to do it, forcing you to do it, or putting it inside you.

It might seem like some people are born driven, and some people are born lazy. While our personality may control some of these behaviors, most of us have to practice motivation. It isn't something you are born into. You have to learn to develop a motivated mindset. You have to learn how to become more motivated, so it becomes easier each time.

Before we talk about strategies to feel more motivated, I want to talk about your motivation style. Knowing this style can help you more easily control your motivation and energy around every task.

FIND YOUR MOTIVATION STYLE

Do you love getting a pat on the back for a job well done? Are you more likely to finish a task if there is a financial reward at the end, like a bonus? Do you get most excited to work on a project if you get to lead the team?

All of these are examples of certain types of motivation styles. Working with students, clients, and teams, I have found that most people fall into one of these motivation styles:

- The Achiever: The achiever is motivated by reaching the goal itself. The excitement of mastery, coupled with a healthy fear of failure, motivate the achiever to push harder when reaching for a goal.
- The Team Member: The team member is motivated by comradery, relationships and affiliation. They like being a valued member of the team. When reaching

for a goal, they are motivated forward by team building and connection.

- The Leader: The leader is motivated by being in power. Leading a team, particularly if there is competition
  with another team, pushes the leader forward toward
  goals. They like to be in charge and like others to look
  to them for guidance.
- The Learner: The learner is motivated by their intrinsic
  curiosity for new and better methods to reach a goal.
  Learning the process is as rewarding as meeting the goal,
  especially if they improve along the way.
- The Winner: The winner is motivated by rewards. Win-
  ners like money, points, rewards, spotlights, and verbal
  appreciation from others.

Why does motivation style matter? When you are looking
to get motivated and stay motivated, knowing your motivation
style allows you to escalate performance like a feedback loop.
Let's look at motivation as a cycle:

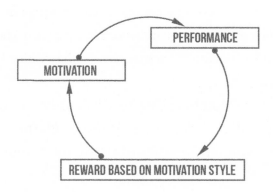

As you begin to perform a task, if you can target the reward based on your motivation style, you become more motivated which leads to better performance. Better performance leads to additional reward and the cycle of motivation continues.

Let's look at an example for the Team Member:

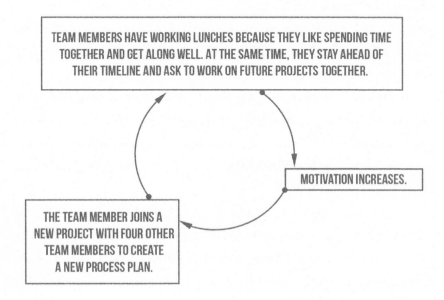

TEAM MEMBERS HAVE WORKING LUNCHES BECAUSE THEY LIKE SPENDING TIME TOGETHER AND GET ALONG WELL. AT THE SAME TIME, THEY STAY AHEAD OF THEIR TIMELINE AND ASK TO WORK ON FUTURE PROJECTS TOGETHER.

MOTIVATION INCREASES.

THE TEAM MEMBER JOINS A NEW PROJECT WITH FOUR OTHER TEAM MEMBERS TO CREATE A NEW PROCESS PLAN.

If you can target how you stay motivated, you can determine how to include those rewards or benefits into the goals you are reaching.

There are other strategies to stay motivated and can work for anyone, no matter your style.

TAKE ACTION

A supermom in motion stays in motion. You must start if you want to keep going. The best strategy to get motivated is just to get started. Do one thing. Don't wait for motivation to strike. Simply take action.

In her book *Better Than Before*, Gretchen Rubin says, "The less we do, the less we feel like doing."[33] The fewer actions we take, the fewer actions we want to take. The less we clean up the house, the less we feel like cleaning up the house. The less we work on our big deadline, the less we feel like working on the big deadline. The less we play with our kids, the less we feel like playing with our kids.

It stands to reason that the more we do something, the more we feel like doing something. Have you ever come home from work and thought, "Ugh. I do not want to make dinner. I do not want to clean up the breakfast dishes from this morning. I just want to do nothing"?

Instead of plunking down on the couch and doing what you are motivated to do, you pick up one pair of shoes from the mudroom. You hang up one jacket. A small step of action helps motivate you to finish the rest of the dinner and the house tasks.

Motivation sparked by "just starting" is another reason I find the morning routine essential to every day. Did you wake up unmotivated? Don't worry. Your habitual morning routine will help you get going, and the resulting motivation will keep you going.

CULTIVATE ENERGY

We talk a lot about energy in this book. You will find it in Chapter 1 when we talk about how habits save mental energy. You will find it in Chapter 5 when we talk about physical energy as a result of a healthy body. You will find it when we talk about rest in

Chapter 10, and you will find it when we talk about finding your energy flow in Chapter 14.

Why is energy so important to being a supermom? The moms I surveyed really struggled with energy. They mentioned exhaustion, being overtired, and lacking energy. They mentioned anxiety, stress, and overwhelm, all of which destroy energy.

Maintaining your level of physical and mental energy to handle stressful situations, busy life activities, and overall happiness is vital to creating your best life.

THE SECRET OF PROXIMITY

In Chapter 15, we dive deep into the "culture of complaint." You will learn how, when you hang out with people that complain, you will tend to complain too. Did you know that you tend to mimic the actions of the people you spend the most time with no matter what they are?

You might have heard that you are the sum of the five people you hang out with most. James Clear says, "We imitate the habits of three groups in particular: The close. The many. The powerful."[34] He is saying that we will act the way those closest to us act. We will

SUPERMOMS HANG OUT WITH SUPERMOMS.

act the way that the majority of the people around us act. We will act the way those in power act.

Put plainly, supermoms hang out with supermoms. If you want to be motivated, have high energy, and live your best life, hang out with other high performers. Find people that have the same goals, values, and motivations that you have for life.

But, you think, *I don't know any people like that.* Find them. Join a networking group. Join a mom's group specifically for working moms. Find other people to put in your proximity that will push you to strive for more.

AVOID BURNOUT

A recent research review on burnout says, "Burnout is a psychological syndrome emerging as a prolonged response to chronic interpersonal stressors on the job. The three key dimensions of this response are an overwhelming exhaustion, feelings of cynicism and detachment from the job, and a sense of ineffectiveness and lack of accomplishment."[35]

Burnout is the enemy of energy and the best friend of overwhelm. If you want to ensure you can maintain adequate energy and motivation, you have to avoid burnout at all costs.

Burnout isn't just for work. You can become burned out on home responsibilities, personal responsibilities, relationships, you name it. The feelings of exhaustion, detachment, and lack of accomplishment can seep into any area of your life.

How do you avoid burnout? Dr. Clark Gaither, family physician and burnout expert, says that the opposite of burnout is *engagement*.[36] He says that vigor, dedication, and absorption are all necessary elements of engagement. When you have these three things, work doesn't feel like work. A job doesn't feel like a job. Responsibilities don't feel like responsibilities.

Write down in your workbook or on a piece of paper a time when you felt engagement. What were you doing? How did it feel? How can you apply that feeling into the work you are doing now at your job or at home?

SUPERMOM SHORTCUT • THE SECRET OF MOTIVATION • CHAPTER WRAP UP

WHAT WE LEARNED

Maintaining motivation and energy is necessary to stay happy and productive. Without motivation, you put yourself at risk for burnout.

HOW WE APPLY IT

First, identify your motivation style. Are you the achiever, the team member, the leader, the learner, or the winner?

After you identify the things that motivate you most and your specific style, use some strategies to stay motivated.

- Take Action: Just. Get. Started.
- Cultivate Energy: Find ways to keep your energy high by controlling mindset, eating well, moving your body, and finding your energy flow.
- The Secret of Proximity: Do you want to be more motivated? Hang out with people that are more motivated than you.
- Avoid Burnout: Find a way to feel engaged with your tasks so they don't feel like work.

ONE SMALL STEP

Just. Get. Started. Do one thing that will move you in the right direction of your goals.

WHAT COMES NEXT

Supermoms can certainly go, go, go. Many moms can do that. The secret supermoms also know is when to *stop*. We will talk about the importance of rest in the next chapter.

CHAPTER 10
SUPERMOMS KNOW WHEN TO STOP

THE SECRET OF REST

"Burnout is nature's way of telling you, you've been going through the motions your soul has departed; you're a zombie, a member of the walking dead, a sleepwalker. False optimism is like administrating stimulants to an exhausted nervous system."

— Sam Keen, *Fire in the Belly: On Being a Man*[37]

"Every person needs to take one day away. A day in which one consciously separates the past from the future. Jobs, family, employers, and friends can exist one day without any one of us, and if our egos permit us to confess, they could exist eternally in our absence. Each person deserves a day away in which no problems are confronted, no solutions searched for. Each of us needs to withdraw from the cares which will not withdraw from us."

— Maya Angelou, *Wouldn't Take Nothing for My Journey Now*[38]

A few years ago, I found my true breaking point.

————————

When I was in high school, I was incredibly busy. I was in Student Council and National Honor Society, and participated in all of our theatre productions. I was no actress but could build a set, create a prop, and organize costumes with the best of them.

I was in all sorts of random clubs, volunteered for a teen suicide hotline, and worked at a clothing store. I graduated fourth in my class in a school with well over two thousand students.

I had a lot going on.

I held near perfect attendance. My parents' rule was that school was your job. You better show up and do your best every single day. Missing school, unless you were violently ill, was never an option.

One day, I lost it. I had a huge project due, and I didn't know how I would get it done. If I just had a few more hours at home to focus and finish, I could get it done. Despite their firm rule, they agreed. I think the fact that I was near hysterical—I almost never cried in general—probably helped.

I didn't make a lot of changes after that, but it did force me to realize that I wasn't completely invincible. I had a point where I could not do and be everything.

My life of involvement, volunteerism, work, and academic achievement continued into college. I went to Arizona State University on a full academic and leadership scholarship. My hard work in high school had paid off and allowed me go to college for free. Much as I would have loved to go to an Ivy League school, the fact that I would leave college debt-free was not lost on me.

I worked full time to pay for food and housing, and I never missed class. I needed little sleep to stay in motion, so I would work midnight to 4:00 a.m. shifts before napping and going to 8:00 a.m. classes.

It might sound like this meant I didn't have a social life, but I had that too. I had friends, went to parties, and took trips to Tucson, Arizona, to see friends from high school. It really felt like I had everything. I was juggling all the balls, and nothing was getting dropped.

I remember the first time I had to pull my car off the freeway. My heart was racing. My chest was tight. I felt like I could barely breathe. I called my parents. They came to take me to my dorm and drive my car home.

That week, I went to the campus medical center. Although I certainly had some weight to lose, otherwise there was nothing wrong with me. It was very likely a panic attack caused by an overwhelmed schedule, lack of sleep, being overweight, college drinking, and eating garbage.

All the balls were in the air, but I wasn't taking time to actually rest for fear of dropping them all. I didn't *have* time. I didn't give myself time to process emotions and filled my time with things to do.

I loved everything I was doing, and I didn't want to lose my activities. But, something obviously had to change.

I decided to get healthier. I cleaned up my eating and drinking and lost twenty pounds. I was still heavier than when I left high school, but I felt much better. The random panic attacks reduced significantly. I could breathe and life was good.

Let's get back to a few years ago. Things were certainly different than they were in college. Since then I had moved to Los Angeles, California, then to Austin, Texas, and back to Phoenix. I went to graduate school at the University of Southern California. I was married, birthed four children, and was ten years into a fast-growing career in clinical research.

Things were good. I was again, as busy as ever.

By this point, I was a master juggler. The balls were in the air, sometimes effortlessly it felt. I had found my sweet spot of "balance." I had habits in place that were working. I was taking care of my health. My body and mind were happy.

Then, I lost control of the whole circus.

It started with a Parent Teacher Association election. I had been a member of the PTA since the school had started. I didn't go to meetings much, but I volunteered for the winter carnival, I brought treats for teacher appreciation week, and I helped where I could.

My motto during this time in my life was that if I *could* say yes, I *would* say yes. If I could go to the school dance and help sell raffle tickets because I was home from a business trip, I would do it. If there was time to use, I would use it. It meant I was busy. It also meant I felt fulfilled. I was helping the school, making my kids happy.

The end of the school year came around, and it was time for the PTA election. The elected board for the previous three years had hit their term limits, and the entire board needed to be replaced. I agreed to come to a meeting because they needed votes.

As they started talking to the other moms, I realized that no one wanted to run the board. No one wanted the responsibility. No one wanted to dedicate the time it required. No one wanted to be tied into this "job" for the next year.

I asked, "What happens if there is no board, if no one runs?"

"Well, the school just won't have a PTA next year."

Wait. Our school was great not only because of the teachers and staff but because of the community that had been built. That community was built in huge part by the events that were hosted by the PTA. No PTA would mean no extra money for school projects, no special treats for teachers, and no activities to bring families together.

I couldn't let that happen, could I?

I walked out the new PTA President.

Four children, a far more than full-time job, a husband who traveled every week, activities for the kids, and now PTA President. I could handle this, right? I was a master juggler.

And then I got promoted.

What. Was. Happening?

I am built to be climbing a career ladder. I am always looking for the next step, learning more, and trying to be better than I was the day before. I had received many promotions before this one, being at the company for so long. A promotion was not a surprise in general.

However, I didn't think this one was coming for at least another year. And it was a big change. I went from overseeing a single team to many teams. My travel was going to increase significantly. It was going to be a challenge, and I knew it.

That next year was one of the hardest of my life. There were days that if I was not infinitely productive from 4:00 a.m. until the second I went to bed, I would fall desperately behind. There were many nights where I barely slept.

I started to hate everything. I had reached maximum burnout. We talked about burnout in the last chapter. Another definition for burnout is "a state of emotional, physical, and mental exhaustion caused by excessive and prolonged stress. It occurs when you feel overwhelmed, emotionally drained, and unable to meet constant demands."[39]

I kept reminding myself that all these stressors were of my own design. That didn't seem to help.

At the end of the year, the expectation was that the board would run for a second term. The bylaws allowed two years in any position, so the natural belief was that members would run again.

I said no.

I almost never said no. Never. I was the one that could make anything happen—and I said no.

I couldn't do it again without losing my mind. I needed to focus on things that brought joy and not only things that were required of me. I needed to see my friends and my husband. I needed date nights.

I made a specific plan for the coming year.

- I would go to concerts. I had not been to live concerts in years, and I loved them! I bought tickets to four concerts—P!nk, The New Kids on the Block, Aerosmith and Korn, in case you are wondering.
- Jeremy and I would go on a date every month. I know some of you are thinking, "What about weekly date night?!?" Nice work for having your marriage top priority. Jeremy and I had slipped to a once every six months or less date night. Monthly seemed more doable and was still a vast improvement.
- We would go on a vacation or stay-cation as a family every quarter.
- I would say yes to friend dates.

That next year was one of the best ever. My friendships were great. My marriage was great. My spirit was great. Let's talk about the importance of rest.

———————

Rest is not sleep. Rest is taking time for yourself to fill your own cup. Have you heard the saying, "You can't pour from an empty cup"? It means that if you don't fulfill yourself, you can't possibly hope to fulfill others.

I had packed my calendar and life so full of jobs and tasks and *stuff* that I had no time for rest. I had not prioritized the things that would fill me up. I had not allowed time in my schedule for the things that would give me energy instead of drain it.

> REST IS NOT SLEEP. REST IS TAKING TIME FOR YOURSELF TO FILL YOUR OWN CUP.

And I knew better. I knew that if I did not actually schedule in periods of rest, they wouldn't happen. I knew that I would squeeze every last drop out of my time bucket and leave no time for me if I didn't force myself to do it.

How do we make sure we get the rest we need?

MAKE A REST LIST

Get out a sheet of paper or pull out your workbook and make a list of *everything* that is rest for you. We previously made a happiness list, and some of those things might fit here too. Still, think about everything that fills you instead of drains you.

Do you love to have dinner with a whole bunch of your best girlfriends? Do you love to curl up with a good book? Do you love to meet your best friend for a glass of wine after you both put your kids to bed or finish a late-night shift? Do you love to meditate? Are you in love with a few shows on Netflix? Maybe you take a Zumba class or yoga? Is a date night in the backyard with your partner what fills you up? Do you feel good after you bawl your eyes out to a sappy romantic comedy? Perhaps you love a massage, or to get your nails done, or a day at the spa?

I want you to write down everything you can think of that is relaxing to you. Obviously, most of us can't afford the time—or money—to go to the spa every day. If it is on the list, though, you can make a priority to schedule one in every month or quarter or year.

SCHEDULE YOUR REST

In order to be the best at managing your time and the efficiency in that time, you must build in rest. You can make it an affirmation or a mantra: *I won't be my best if I don't get my rest.*

Look at your calendar and actually schedule the times that you will *intentionally* rest. Notice that this is rest taken on purpose. This is not randomly taking a few minutes to scroll social media and having it turn into an hour lost. This is not flopping into bed after tucking in the kids and saying, "Now I am just going to rest for a little while before I finish the laundry and the dinner dishes and my last report for work."

When you are planning your time for rest, decide how often you will need it. Really think about what will make you the best in your life.

Do you need twenty minutes every day to meditate? Does one night out with friends or your partner a week give you the energy you need? What will make you feel like you are taking care of yourself in the best way?

What will help you *engage* with your life instead of feel burned out by it?

GO ALL IN

I asked one of my girlfriends if she was ever taking time for herself.

"Well, I watch Netflix three nights a week while I am folding laundry." Can you see my snarled-up face?

Rest is not multitasking. It isn't getting in a little bit of something you like—in this case, Netflix—while getting a task or a chore done—in this case, laundry. Would you take a business meeting while getting a massage? No—well, most of us, no.

When you are taking your rest time, you are going to "go all in." If you decide that the most relaxing thing for you is a forty-minute show on Netflix, you are going to *only watch Netflix*. You are going to luxuriate in this time that is only for you. Is it eating a piece of chocolate cake? Just you and the cake and bliss. No distractions.

This full, deliberate focus on the pleasure of the joyful activity you have chosen is the only way for it to actually be restful for you.

DON'T BREAK PROMISES TO YOURSELF

Your rest is yours. No one is going to make you take it. If you decide to skip your rest to take on another task, no one will know. But, you will know. Eventually, it will lead you to bitterness and to burnout.

You might need to force yourself to start. If you are not used to focusing on just what you need to be better, it might feel weird. You might feel guilty. You might feel selfish.

Those are tough feelings. They can make you want to stop. Know that you deserve to take care of yourself. Know that you will feel better and actually *be* better, so much better, when you do.

THE FIVE-MINUTE REST

Did you forget to schedule rest today? Did your day turn out unexpectedly and you need a way to de-stress quickly? Do you need just five minutes to yourself?

You *could* lock yourself in the bathroom and cry. Sometimes you need that.

If your time is short but you really need to feel refreshed, here are my five favorite ways to induce a feeling of rest in five minutes or less, no tears required. You can do them sitting on the couch, laying on your bed, or hiding in your closet. Again, you do you.

THE HYPNO-BREATHING REST

The hypno-breathing rest is my favorite way to get fully relaxed in just minutes. When I was pregnant with Kinley, I decided I wanted to have a medication-free birth, if possible. After researching several options, I opted to take a hypnobirthing class.

During that class we learned a bunch of techniques, but I only used one. I used that same one to deliver all four of my babies without pain medication. I promise, if it works for *labor*, it will certainly work for whatever stressful day you have encountered.

Sit in a still and comfortable position—I like to have my palms faced up, but you do you. Slowly inhale, focusing on your stomach. You want it to feel like you are very slowly blowing up your abdomen like a balloon. Fast count while you do it, until you can inhale no more. 1,2,3,4,5,6,7,8,9,10,11,12….

When I am really good at this, I can get to thirty or forty before my balloon is "full."

Then, exhale just as slowly as you inhaled, fast counting again. Try to blow out every bit of the air in your body. Your goal is to exhale to the same number. So, if you inhaled and fast counted up to twenty-one, try to exhale to twenty-one also.

Repeat several times in a row, each time focusing only on the slowness of your breath and the fast counting.

If you practice this one, you will start to feel incredibly relaxed at even the first inhale. It is powerful and fast.

THE ANTI-ANXIETY REST

When I was in graduate school for marriage and family therapy, I took a class from a famous psychiatry professor. The class was on cognitive behavioral therapy. She was tough, but she was amazing.

The class walked in one night, super stressed about a big test. You could tell that the entire class was on edge. The test was a big one, and everyone knew that it could make or break their grade. Her tests were *hard*, and being overly anxious was not helping anyone in the class.

She asked everyone to sit. Then, she told us to put everything on the floor. We were all confused at this point.

She told us to close our eyes. We trusted her, so we did. Then, she walked us through the following exercise.

"I want you to focus on your breathing. Just think about your breathing. You are going to fill your lungs with air, and then blow it out slowly. Inhale…"

She counted slowly from one to eight. "1…..2…..3…..4…..5…..6…..7…..8….."

"Exhale…" Again, she counted slowly to eight.

She repeated the slow inhale and exhale about four times in a row. Then, she asked us to open our eyes, pick up our books from the floor, and begin our exam.

I got an A on that test.

THE BODY RELAXATION REST

This is a favorite technique that I learned from one of my college professors. Sitting or lying in a still position, you will start with your feet. Focus only on your feet, make them tense, and then relax them as much as you possibly can.

Spend ten to twenty seconds just relaxing your feet. Then, move up to your calves. Again, spend ten to twenty seconds thinking only of your calves, make them tense, and then relax as much as you can.

You will move up your entire body, tensing and then relaxing each body part, all the way up to your head.

By the time you reach the top, you should feel relaxation in all parts of your body.

THE VISUALIZATION REST

Visualization is used in many arenas. It is used by the highest achievers, yogis, athletes, and those who are setting big goals. It is used by CEOs and speakers. In his book *The Seven Habits of Highly Successful People*, Stephen Covey even touts it as one of the critical seven habits[40]. He calls it "beginning with the end in mind." It can be extraordinarily powerful.

I like this type of rest when I know I am about to lose my mind. Whereas high performers use visualization to see themselves doing great things, I use visualization to see myself using great restraint.

When I can feel myself at a breaking point, a point where I want to scream at the kids, I use this technique. When I can feel like the next conversation will be hard, I use this technique. When I feel like I have a big chance of losing my cool, I use this technique.

Visualization is seeing yourself doing something in your mind. It isn't just a quick run through of what you are going to say when you walk out of your office door. It is actually walking through your entire interaction, every thought, every feeling.

For example, let's say the kids have decided to play six different games, and they are all now mixed and strewn about the living room floor. You are trying to finish an unexpected business call and get dinner started.

You might be tempted to scream at the kids, to scream at your partner, or to be short with your colleague.

Here is where you stop. Stop for five minutes, and see yourself the way you want to act in the situation. See yourself in your mind calmly talking to your kids. Walk through the entire inter-action in vivid detail. Think about exactly what you will say. Vis-ualize how you will feel, what the room will look and smell like, your feelings of relaxation and calm as you lovingly interact with your children.

Your hands are soft not clenched. Your voice is even, not screaming. You end the discussion calm as your children begin to clean up the vast mess of Monopoly money and Candyland figurines.

Visualization can allow you to see your life the way you want to live it, reach goals, and interact with others as your best self. It also allows the pause before you act out of frustration instead of love.

THE ACTIVE REST

Finally, another favorite and fast rest technique is the active rest. I call this active rest because you are actually moving your body, unlike the other forms of rest we discussed.

Have you ever noticed how amazing it feels to stretch when you wake up in the morning? Kids do it. Pets do it. We do it.

Why do you think that might be? When you stretch, you re-duce muscle tension, increase blood flow throughout your body, and reduce stress. In addition, you activate your parasympathet-ic nervous system and release endorphins.[41]

What does all this mean? Your parasympathetic nervous sys-tem tells your body it is time to relax. Endorphins are chemicals that tell our brain we should feel happy or euphoric. When you stretch, you feel relaxed and happy. A relaxed and happy mom is a rested mom.

How can you do this in five minutes? Stand up and notice where you feel tension in your body. Is it your neck and shoulders? Is it your legs? Your feet?

Notice where you feel the most tension and start there, move around, and do what feels good. Does it feel good to stretch your arms way over your head? Do that. Does it feel good to touch your toes? Do that.

Arm circles, shoulder raises, head rolls, calf raises, and so many more movements might feel good in that specific moment. For five minutes, spend time doing whatever feels the best for your body, focusing only on the stretching and incredible feelings within.

SUPERMOM SHORTCUT • THE SECRET OF REST • CHAPTER WRAP UP

WHAT WE LEARNED

Rest is critical to avoiding burnout and staying engaged in both work and home. When we fail to schedule rest into our already busy calendars, we are unlikely to take it. When we don't prioritize intentional rest, we risk exhaustion, cynicism, and feelings of reduced capability.

HOW WE APPLY IT

In order to make sure you rest every day or week, you must first know what is rest *for you*. Make a list of things that relax you and make you happy. Then, schedule those things, and put them in your actual calendar. Schedule the time and make it non-negotiable. Focus only on your restful activity and don't break the promise to yourself that you will take it.

ONE SMALL STEP

In just five minutes, you can use one of the techniques in this chapter to quickly recharge. Try one of the following:

- The Hypno-Breathing Rest
- The Anti-Anxiety Rest
- The Body Relaxation Rest
- The Visualization Rest
- The Active Rest

WHAT COMES NEXT

As the final wrap up of the secrets of body and mind, we will talk about mindset. In this chapter, we will discuss the ability to grow and how to release guilt.

CHAPTER 11
SUPERMOMS BELIEVE THEY WILL SUCCEED

THE SECRET OF MINDSET

> "When you change the way you look at things, the things you look at change."
>
> — Dr. Wayne Dyer

> "In the fixed mindset, everything is about the outcome. If you fail—or if you're not the best—it's all been wasted. The growth mindset allows people to value what they're doing regardless of the outcome. They're tackling problems, charting new courses, working on important issues. Maybe they haven't found the cure for cancer, but the search was deeply meaningful."
>
> — Carol S. Dweck, *Mindset: The New Psychology of Success*[42]

When I was going to be a senior in high school, I ran for Student Body President. I had been elected the president of the sophomore and junior class. I loved my school, I was a walking, talking picture of school spirit, and I was smart and organized. It would only make sense that I should run for president of the whole student body.

I made all the posters and hung them around campus. I wrote my speech on everything I would do to make the campus better. I talked to friends and acquaintances every morning before school. I did everything to ensure a win.

I lost.

I decided to run for Senior Class President. I knew I could do better. I made new posters. I made sure everyone I knew would be sure to vote. I wrote my message to the class.

I lost again.

At this point, in order to be part of the council, the only option was to apply for a Member at Large position. The Member at Large was a position that required an application to a committee. The application required an essay on how you would benefit the school and why you should be part of the council.

I knew I could do this. I was not going to let failures prevent me from being part of Student Council for my last year of high school. I had been a member every year. I put all my heart and soul into that essay. I asked teachers to review my essay. I took all the feedback I could in order to make sure I would be chosen.

They picked me.

I could have easily given up after losing the election for Student Body President. I could have thought, *I guess I am not good enough to be president this year*. I could have thought, *I guess no one likes me enough this year*. I could have thought I was not popular enough or smart enough or pretty enough or a good enough president in the past.

I could have run again and just kept my election materials the same instead of learning how I could do better. I could have done everything alone without getting constructive feedback from others.

Instead, I pushed through the challenges, made changes, got feedback, and got to work. My mindset was a key driver in pushing forward.

———————

What is mindset? Mindset is a grouping of attitudes or beliefs that define us. A positive mindset encourages a habit of positive attitude and looks for the best in any situation.

ARE YOU GROWING?

Another way to look at mindset was made popular by Carol S. Dweck, a Stanford psychologist, in 2007.[43] Dr. Dweck divides mindset into two groups. In any particular area, people may have a growth mindset or a fixed mindset.

A growth mindset is believing your talents in any area can be developed. They are learned. A fixed mindset is believing that you are born with specific talents or skills. They are innate.

As an example, let's pretend I just completed a work presentation. I stuttered, forgot part of my presentation, read directly from my slides, and overall presented poorly. I could decide that I am just a terrible public speaker (fixed mindset), or I could decide that I have not perfected public speaking skills *yet* (growth mindset).

With a fixed mindset, I am unlikely to try to get better at speaking. I am unlikely to practice or look for ways to improve.

With a growth mindset, I might schedule a class on public speaking. I would look for ways to practice over the next few months. I would experiment with different speaking methods.

You may have both a fixed and a growth mindset, depending on the topic. For example, I have a growth mindset when it comes to parenting and my career. I believe that I can learn new skills and strive to get better every day. I know that I won't be great at everything but can develop as a mom.

However, when it comes to sports, I have a fixed mindset. I believe that I am terrible at sports. I will never get better no matter how hard I try—and so I never try.

Could I get better at golf or basketball or catching a ball of any sort? I probably could. If I practiced, I certainly could be no worse than I am today. I don't try because I set a belief long ago that I was not athletic and bad at sports—like, really bad. Please never throw anything to me and expect me to catch it.

A fixed mindset might show up in a number of ways:

- You believe that your talents, your intelligence, and your abilities are innate. You believe this of others as well. If you weren't born good at math, you will never be good at math.
- You avoid challenges. You have never taken a Zumba class because you are a horrible dancer. You are bound to be horrible. You don't believe you will get better, so why try?

- You don't listen to constructive feedback or criticism, even when it is helpful. Your boss provides a really good resource to help you get better at selling after a botched bid defense. You just aren't a born saleswoman.
- You give up easily. You tried to potty train your three-year-old, but it didn't work after a day. You just weren't meant to potty train kids. Your husband will have to do it.
- You feel threatened by others when they succeed. It's not fair that Bob got all the brains. Everything is just easy for him.
- You focus on the result instead of the process. You got laid off, so that must mean you were never meant to be an engineer.

Think about areas where you have a fixed mindset, like my sports belief. It certainly isn't serving me. Where might your mindset be holding you back or not serving you in some way?

A growth mindset, on the other hand, focuses on just that: growth. Moms with a growth mindset believe they can succeed and even enjoy the process of getting better. A growth mindset might look like this:

- You believe that some people are born with certain talents, abilities, and smarts, but these things can also be improved. With practice and focus, you can get better, smarter, and faster. The first cake you decorated was abysmal, a true Pinterest fail, but you are confident you can start a business if you practice the skills.

- You are fired up by challenges. You get excited to learn something new. Salsa dancing tonight? Never tried it, but sounds fun!
- You know that you will not be perfect on the first try and accept criticism. Oh, her diaper is on backwards? Now I know for next time!
- You can push forward through adversity or failure. Well, the interview did not go as I planned, and I didn't get the job. I am going to practice my responses and apply for more jobs tomorrow.
- You enjoy the process. You like the trial and error of getting to the other side of a challenge. I can do better, let's run through the pitch again.
- You are inspired by others. Wow, Jenni was promoted three times in the last three years! She must be doing something right. I am going to ask if she will mentor me.

Supermoms don't let challenges hold them back at work, and they don't let challenges hold them back at home. They believe they can be better moms and better at their careers. They believe that they can get anything they want if they work hard and figure out how to get there.

They teach their children that they can get better at things, too, with practice and grit.

A WORD ABOUT GUILT

One of the biggest struggles of moms, especially working moms, is guilt. Brene Brown defines guilt as "... holding something we've done or failed to do up against our values and feeling psychological discomfort."[44]

Often as moms, we aren't even feeling guilty for valid reasons. We are at work and feeling guilty for not being home, even though we are providing for our family and showing our children what moms can achieve. We are at home and feeling guilty for not working more even though we hit a big deadline and worked a sixty-hour week. We are feeling this discomfort when we know it isn't rational.

> LETTING GO OF GUILT AND THE GUILT MINDSET IS THE ONLY PATH TO BECOMING A HAPPY SUPERMOM.

Letting go of guilt and the guilt mindset is the only path to becoming a happy supermom. As with other negative emotions, guilt can increase health issues, depression, and anxiety.

What are some tangible ways to let go of guilt?

FORGIVENESS

Forgiveness can allow a weight to be lifted off your shoulders. Forgiveness is not only reserved for others. Forgiving yourself is a critical part of letting go of guilt.

Did you miss the first day of Kindergarten, but Dad was there and the day went great? Forgive yourself. Did you miss the big game but he can't wait to show you the video of him scoring the winning goal? Forgive yourself. Is she still really angry that you have to miss the show? Apologize, love on her, and forgive yourself.

DO A VALUES CHECK

In the next chapter, we will review setting priorities. We'll dive deep into discovering what is truly the most important to you.

Are you feeling guilty because you have slipped on your priorities? Taking a look at what you value most, a values check, can be useful in getting to the root of the guilt. You can then either make some changes or let it go.

The easiest way to do a quick values check is a values pie. Put the ten most important things in your life as each piece of the pie. Need to add more? Add more, but I like ten. Take your pie and number each item from one to ten with one being the most important. Now, look at your priorities and the way you spend your time each week. Are they aligned? If not, it is time for a reset so your tasks line up with your values.

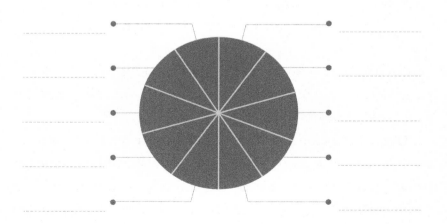

ASK FOR HELP

We all need help at some point. No one goes through life alone and can do it all. If you are feeling guilty, ask for help, delegate tasks, or start to outsource.

THE BIG PICTURE

Sometimes it is important to just take a big step back. Zoom way out on your life, and look at it with the perspective of an astronaut. You are floating above the earth with your giant astronaut head, weightless in your spacesuit.

What do you see when you are floating in space far above your life?

Does it actually look pretty awesome? Do you see a strong, capable mom raising independent, well-adjusted kids? Do you have a career you love, a family you love, and a relationship you love? Do you see a healthy mom with healthy kids? Do you see smiles and joy?

What if it doesn't look like that at all? If you take a big zoom out on your life and the view is not pretty, it is time to go back to your values. It is time for some changes.

REMEMBER…YOU ARE ENOUGH

Guilt can often come from not feeling like you are "enough." Not home enough, not a good enough boss, not a good enough cook, not a good enough partner, not a good enough mom.

Stop.

You. Are. Enough.

If you didn't add "I am enough" to your list of affirmations from Chapter 2, go back and add that one now.

SUPERMOM SHORTCUT • THE SECRET OF MINDSET • CHAPTER WRAP UP

WHAT WE LEARNED

Mindset is the belief that you will grow and get better instead of allow your innate talents to limit your success. Mindset also allows you to release guilt and look at the big picture.

HOW WE APPLY IT

Determine areas in your life where you may have a fixed mindset. How is this limiting your ability to succeed and grow? Can you adopt a growth mindset and challenge yourself to get better?

Supermoms also know that a guilt mindset will ultimately destroy their happiness and their success. In order to let go of guilt, try some of these techniques:

- Forgive
- Do a Values Check
- Ask for Help
- Look at the Big Picture
- Remember…You Are Enough

ONE SMALL STEP

For the next five minutes, take a look at your life from a 10,000-foot view. What stands out? Is it amazing? Keep doing what you are doing. Can you find parts that are not working? Time to set some priorities.

WHAT COMES NEXT

Our final section of this book reviews secret skills that super-moms develop over time to do things better, faster, and happier. The most amazing part is that anyone can learn these skills. We will start with setting priorities.

PART 3

THE SECRET SKILLS

CHAPTER 12
SUPERMOMS KNOW
THE MOST IMPORTANT THING

THE SECRET OF SETTING PRIORITIES

"Things which matter most must never be at the mercy of
things which matter least."
— Johann Wolfgang von Goethe

"There is no such thing as 'I do not have the time.' This is all just
a matter of priorities."
— Maciej Aniserowicz

"Wow! You're a really bad mom."
He was smiling, and I knew he was kidding, but I couldn't help but let it roll around in my head.

We had just finished the first day of a week-long meeting in Boston, Massachusetts. It was a six-hour flight back to Phoenix, so I would not be back home until the meeting was over. That meant missing opening night of my oldest daughter's theatre production.

I never missed opening night.

We had a tradition. I would come to the first night, alone. Just me in the audience, so I could focus all of my attention and adoration on her. I would bring her flowers. She would pretend to be surprised even though she would remind me to buy them.

The second night, I would come to see the show again. This time, I would bring Jeremy and the other kids. If anyone needed to go to the bathroom or freaked out for any reason, I could step out without missing a key part of the show. I had been there the first night, after all.

This was her tenth production, and we had never broken this tradition.

As the meeting wrapped up, I pulled out my phone. I was getting ready to call her and wish her the obligatory "break a leg" before we headed out for the mandatory client dinner. As I did, I shared our tradition with my co-worker.

"Wow! You're a really bad mom."

Ouch.

I laughed it off. I knew he was kidding. I knew he traveled way more often than I did and missed far more weekly activities with his own kids.

Still, the tease hit hard. Was I a bad mom? I *had* never missed a birthday. But, I had missed choir concerts and baseball practice. I had missed Kami's first day of Kindergarten, the other kids' first day of school that year—and now this.

Did that make me a bad mom? Would it make him a bad dad?

———————

Setting priorities is a critical skill of any supermom. There will always be an overflow of work expectations, parenting expectations, relationship expectations, social expectations, and the list goes on. Everyone will want all of your time. Everyone will have an opinion about how you choose to spend it.

In this chapter, I want to provide you some concrete strategies for setting priorities because it can be really hard. First, though, I want you to just make a list of everything that is most important to you. Right now.

Just make a list. Pull out a piece of paper or get out your Secrets of Supermom Workbook and write down the ten most important things to you off the top of your head. Don't think. Just write. If you did the values activity from the last chapter, you could pull that out.

Here is what happens when you do this exercise without planning and without time to make your grand list of all things important. You find the most important things. You find, in your heart of hearts, what means the most to you.

No matter what you are trying to prioritize, keep that list close. As you work through some of these other activities, it can serve as your beacon when your ship feels like it is going off course. Go back to those key priorities so you remember what is most important.

Not all prioritizing efforts are the same. Every strategy won't work in every situation. Your go-to "number your priorities from one to ten" doesn't always give you the results that you need to feel good about next steps. It doesn't always feel right.

In the next sections, we will look at different strategies when you are looking to the future, when you have to make a choice, when you just simply have too many things to do, when there are too many options, and finally, when things feel out of control.

WHEN YOU ARE MAKING PLANS FOR YOUR FUTURE

What are your big dreams? Start a company, have another baby, take a safari in Africa, become CEO, get a degree, have a once a week date night, get married, open a bookstore? All of these?

In order to decide where to put your efforts—and *succeed* with them—you have to be able to prioritize all the audacious dreams and big goals.

There is a story about a philosophy professor. He stands at the front of his class with a jar and fills it with some rocks. He asks if the jar is full. The students say, "Yes."

He progressively fills the jar with pebbles, sand, and finally water, each time asking if the jar is full, and each time the class agreeing that the jar is full.

His intention is to show that you may always have space to add more to your life, to your task list. However, if you put in water first, the least important stuff in this metaphor, you have no room for what is most important.

Focus on the rocks. Prioritize the rocks.

If you are looking to your future, either alone or with a business partner or with your family, determine those big goals. Are they one-year goals, five-year goals, ten-year goals? If you don't determine the most important plans for your future and allow them to become the priorities, you will never reach those big goals.

You have to decide, either alone or with your team or family, which goals to pursue. You have to choose the rocks. You also have to choose what is less important and can be put on the backburner until a better time or later date.

Don't allow the sand and the water to displace the rocks.

WHEN YOU HAVE TO MAKE A CHOICE

Sometimes prioritizing comes down to making a choice, and that choice is hard. It might just suck altogether.

Let's go back to my story about my daughter and her opening night for her show. I obviously made a choice to be in Boston at a business meeting instead of in Phoenix at her show. Why?

How did I decide to prioritize work over my child?

It sounds pretty painful when I put it that way, doesn't it? It sounds like my job is more important than my child.

This is exactly what guilt and blame and the illusion of balance do to us. You *will* have to make hard choices. If you want to succeed in your career, your business, your side hustle, there *will* be times when schedules overlap and a choice must be made.

Is my family my priority? 100%. Is the strength and support of my team also my priority? 100%.

How did I decide?

When I have to make a hard choice, my strategy is a simple pros and cons list. You don't have to write the list down. You might just want to talk it out with your boss, your coach, your partner, or your best friend.

In my case, I went through each scenario. What would be the benefits, and what would be the consequences?

What were the pros of attending Kinley's show?

- She will feel supported and loved.
- Our tradition will be maintained.
- I will see the first show (something I do truly love).
- I won't have to take a red-eye flight to Boston and excel on limited sleep.
- I won't spend eighteen hours traveling on multiple flights that week.

How about the cons?

- I will miss critical parts of my business meeting.
- My team will run the meeting alone without the benefit of sidebars, body language, and eye contact from me.
- My client will be irritated by my lack of presence.
- I will miss team building via dinners and in-person team building activities.

What were the pros of attending the business meeting?

- My team will get to meet with me early in the morning before the start of the meeting.
- My team will get a face-to-face debrief of the meeting to decide next-day strategy.
- My client will feel supported, happy, and important.

- I will get a face-to-face chat with the vice president of my department.
- I will get to attend all the team dinners and bonding experiences to solidify our teamwork plan.
- Jeremy and the kids will get to go to opening night, something they had never done, since it was always reserved for me.
- Jeremy will get to surprise Kinley with flowers since they would not be expected from him.
- Jeremy will understand the importance of opening night. As a theatre girl in high school, I certainly understood performances. Jeremy had never performed so didn't really "get it." This was not a pro for him necessarily, but certainly was for me.
- All of my kids will get to see what it looks like to be a successful mommy, working hard despite missed events and bummer situations.
- I could still catch the last show when I returned from the meeting in Boston—barring any significant flight delays—and get a video of opening night.

How about the cons?

- I will miss the first show, something that definitely bums me out.
- Kinley might be disappointed in the change of plans.

- Jeremy will have to do "all the things" including costume prep, makeup, hair, and maintaining the other children while prepping the little actress.
- I will have to travel many hours and endure overnights on a plane.
- I will spend four nights away from my family.

After looking at all the options, attending the meeting was a better choice than missing it. Both work and family are unbelievably important to me. Simply put, the consequences of not attending the show could be easily remedied. The consequences of not attending the meeting, not as much. The choice was difficult, but it was obvious.

Using a pros and cons list can help you make a choice when one option is not a higher priority than the other, but a choice is required.

WHEN YOU HAVE TOO MANY THINGS TO DO

We have all felt it. We have all been there. A to-do list with ninety-nine tasks and no way to make it through them all. How do we even start?

My favorite way to determine what really needs to get done versus what is less important is using a chart, often referred to as the Eisenhower Decision Matrix.

Draw a big plus sign on a piece of paper creating four boxes or quadrants. Divide those quadrants into urgent versus not urgent and important versus not important. Your chart will look something like the diagram below or use your Secrets of Super-mom Workbook for a pre-created matrix.

URGENT, IMPORTANT	NOT URGENT, IMPORTANT
URGENT, NOT IMPORTANT	NOT URGENT, NOT IMPORTANT

You will evaluate every task on your list, and put it into one of the four buckets. Here are some examples of what types of tasks would go into each bucket:

URGENT, IMPORTANT	NOT URGENT, IMPORTANT
○ Erupting crises ○ Projects with impending due dates ○ Last-minute requests ○ Angry clients ○ Illness	○ Strategy sessions ○ Relationship building ○ Health activities ○ Research ○ Long-term goal setting

URGENT, NOT IMPORTANT	NOT URGENT, NOT IMPORTANT
○ Interruptions ○ Daily tasks ○ Some meetings ○ Low value tasks ○ Travel planning	○ Busy work ○ Time-wasters (More on terrible time-wasters in Chapter 13) ○ Trivial tasks ○ Junk mail

Take every task and put it into a bucket. Here are some examples of what the matrix might look like for work and home:

THE HOME MATRIX

URGENT, IMPORTANT	NOT URGENT, IMPORTANT
○ Doctor's appointment for sick child ○ A hungry baby ○ Agenda for a club meeting you are hosting tonight ○ Shopping for tonight's dinner ○ A burning smell	○ Planning date night with husband ○ Setting family budget to save for a pool ○ Your yoga class ○ Vacation research for your next big trip ○ Meal planning
URGENT, NOT IMPORTANT	**NOT URGENT, NOT IMPORTANT**
○ Paying bills ○ Responding to emails for other people's needs ○ Cleaning up breakfast dishes ○ Church meeting that lasts ninety minutes but scheduled for thirty	○ Refiling tax documents after your meeting with your CPA ○ Social media black holes ○ Sorting junk mail ○ Watching TV ○ Pointless text messages

THE WORK MATRIX

URGENT, IMPORTANT	NOT URGENT, IMPORTANT
○ An angry client with a botched order ○ A presentation slide deck for this afternoon ○ A project due tonight ○ A sick team member with a deadline due today	○ Meeting with a potential client ○ Networking meetings ○ Creating a standard operating procedure for your social media rollout ○ Planning out Q2 goals

URGENT, NOT IMPORTANT	NOT URGENT, NOT IMPORTANT
○ Scheduling your business trip for Monday ○ A last-minute meeting called by your boss ○ Pulling together reports for someone else ○ Making copies for an upcoming meeting ○ An interruption into your office	○ Organizing emails into folders ○ Watercooler gossip ○ Unnecessary phone calls ○ Internet shopping ○ Re-sorting media files ○ Changing your desktop background

Once all of your tasks are in their respective quadrants, you can start to manage them. You will start with the urgent and important tasks.

Urgent and important tasks need your immediate attention. These often are tasks that only you can do or that you need to do right away and have no time to delegate—like a kitchen fire or angry client who is at the front desk. The goal is to keep this quadrant small and managed. We can't prevent sick children or always prevent angry clients, but if we are constantly spending time in the urgent and important, we have no time to plan for the things that are most important in our lives.

Ideally, you will get to a point where most of your time is spent on the *important but not urgent items*. This means that you are managing your time, you are working on tasks that actually move the needle, and you are allowing yourself time to plan and strategize. These tasks bring you the most fulfillment and lead you to a long-term goal.

Using examples from the table above, *important but not urgent* tasks at home are things like date night. Date night, while not urgent, increases the quality of your relationship in the long term. Planning your second quarter goals at work leads you to workplace fulfillment.

Urgent but not important tasks are those that must be done, but don't need to be done by you. Are you the only person that can pay bills at your house or can you delegate or set up auto-pay? Are you the only person that can schedule your business trip or can you have a travel agent or assistant do that for you?

One way to manage these urgent but truly unimportant tasks is to delegate them to a team member, a family member, an assistant, or someone else you hire. Your other option is to do your best to minimize them—interruptions, for example—or automate them. These tasks still must get done, but they don't necessarily need to be done by you.

The final bucket of tasks are the *non-urgent and not important* tasks. These are often the terrible time-wasters talked about in the next chapter. Checking social media for the fifth time, organizing things for the sake of organizing—not to make life truly easier—procrastinating, and watching TV all fall into this bucket. For these tasks, your goal is to eliminate them as much as possible. Need thirty minutes of TV to decompress? Schedule it purposefully, and don't allow it to turn into three hours of mindlessness.

WHEN THERE ARE TOO MANY OPTIONS

Last summer, we decided to build a pool. Our backyard had been average for twelve years, and it was time for an upgrade. We met with six local companies. Each company met with us at our home, provided us with a proposed design, and provided a planned budget.

Now, we had to make a decision. Jeremy and I tend to lean to the logical side, especially Jeremy. There were simply too many factors and too many options to just make a choice. One company simply didn't jump out as the best choice from the start.

In order to help us make our final decision, and feel good about it, we used the ranking method. We decided that the three key factors of choice were pool design, budget, and company we would like to work with. The company rating took into account the feeling we got about the company, the desire to work with the sales representative who met with us, and our overall understanding of what was in each package.

We each rated the factors from one to six separately. It looked something like this:

DESIGN	BUDGET	COMPANY
4 Pool Company A	6 Pool Company A	6 Pool Company A
1 Pool Company B	2 Pool Company B	1 Pool Company B
6 Pool Company C	5 Pool Company C	5 Pool Company C
5 Pool Company D	4 Pool Company D	4 Pool Company D
2 Pool Company E	1 Pool Company E	3 Pool Company E
3 Pool Company F	3 Pool Company F	2 Pool Company F

Once we completed our rankings, we put them together with point values. Immediately four companies were off the table. It allowed us to quickly narrow down too many options to a manageable two choices.

WHEN THINGS FEEL OUT OF CONTROL

Sometimes things are just simply overwhelming. There are too many responsibilities and not enough time to do them. We feel like things are spinning out of control.

A similar strategy to the ranking method is coined by Brian Tracy and called the ABCDE Method.[45] He suggests writing down everything you need to do. Brain dump *all of it* into a long list of tasks and activities.

With that list, rank each item with an A (super important), B (less important), C (nice to have), D (could be delegated or skipped), and E (unimportant and could be eliminated altogether).

Once your rankings are complete, group all A's together, B's together, and so on. You will then rank those in order to create an A1, A2, A3, and so on.

This method allows you to quickly find the most important tasks and decide where to start (at A1) and move through the list accordingly.

THE MOST IMPORTANT THING

Before we close out this chapter, I want to tell you that setting priorities is not always easy. The tools above definitely help to make things easier, but sometimes the choices will be really tough.

Missing my daughter's opening night, despite knowing it was the right choice, was hard. Missing the first day of Kindergarten was hard. My family is a priority, but it doesn't mean they get 100% of me. It doesn't mean the family choice will always win out.

Here are a few more keys to help keep priorities clear, especially when it comes to family.

- Quality over Quantity: My kids do not get 100% of me. My husband does not get 100% of me. When we are together, I focus on quality time because the quantity of time won't always be there. I focus on it so much that the kids

MY KIDS DO NOT GET 100% OF ME. MY HUSBAND DOES NOT GET 100% OF ME. WHEN WE ARE TOGETHER, I FOCUS ON QUALITY TIME BECAUSE THE QUANTITY OF TIME WON'T ALWAYS BE THERE.

like to say, "Mommy *makes* us do fun stuff." Well, lucky them.

- Stay Connected: I am not sure what I would do without FaceTime. Video calling with my husband and children has been a lifesaver when I am at a late meeting or away on a business trip. It allowed Jeremy to stay connected to the kids all those years he traveled every week. Find a way to stay connected when you can't be physically present.

- Know When to Say *No*: You have to know when to just say *no*. *No* to the business trip or the speaking engagement or the extra client meeting. *No* to the volunteer request or the church responsibility or the girls' night out. You have to know when your family just needs *you* and when to put them first.

SUPERMOM SHORTCUT • THE SECRET SETTING PRIORITIES • CHAPTER WRAP UP

WHAT WE LEARNED

Supermoms know that setting priorities is critical to getting the most from career, relationships, and life. If we don't set priorities, we say yes to things that are not aligned with our long-term goals, we neglect our families, and we get overwhelmed.

HOW WE APPLY IT

In this chapter, you will find several strategies to set priorities to reach your overall goals as well as for your task list.

- Decide on your long-term goals and focus on the most important steps to those goals (the rocks) instead of allowing minor tasks, busy work, and unimportant minutia get in the way (the water).
- Use a pros and cons list when a decision must be made between two high-priority activities.
- Use a decision matrix to determine what is urgent, what is important, and what simply is not. Use this tool to decide where to start and determine what tasks can be delegated or eliminated.
- Use a ranking system, like assigning point values, to help make a choice. This is especially helpful when making a decision with your partner or with a team.
- If you are overwhelmed, use the ABCDE Method to determine the most important and least important tasks so you know where to start.

ONE SMALL STEP

Brain dump all the things you need to do today, this week, and this month onto a piece of paper or into your workbook. Then, when you are ready, choose a strategy from this chapter to rank those tasks and get them done.

WHAT COMES NEXT

Setting priorities is a supermom skill. Once you know that is most important, you can dive into time management and using that time to be productive. We will talk about time-management strategies in the next chapter.

CHAPTER 13
SUPERMOMS ALWAYS HAVE TIME

THE SECRET OF TIME MANAGEMENT

"If it's your job to eat a frog, it's best to do it first thing in the morning. And if it's your job to eat two frogs, it's best to eat the biggest one first."
— Attributed to Mark Twain

"The hours don't suddenly appear. You have to steal them from comfort."
— Derek Sivers[46]

"Discipline is the whole key to being successful. We all get 24 hours each day. That's the only fair thing; it's the only thing that's equal. What we do with those 24 hours is up to us."
— Sam Huff, NFL Football Player[47]

"How do you get so many things done all the time?" she asked me. It wasn't one of those "I don't know how you do it" flyaway comments. She was serious.

"I don't know. If I want to get it all done, I just do it, I guess."

"Yeah, but how are you not awake until 3:00 a.m. and stressed out all the time?"

"Well, I decide what I am going to do and when I am going to do it—and then I do it."

It seemed so simple, but I knew it wasn't. I knew she wasn't the only mom struggling with managing time and getting things done.

In creating this book, I informally surveyed and interviewed hundreds of moms. I have talked with moms for years about their struggles and their frustrations. The problem they almost always tell me is not having enough time. They feel like they don't have time to balance all of life's priorities: partner, family, work, school, church, friends, fun.

Sound familiar?

- "I just can't seem to balance it all."
- "I wish I had more time to get things done."
- "I feel like I am on a hamster wheel where I have been running all day. I get to the end of my day and am in the same place I started. The house is a disaster, I am no closer to reaching my deadline, and I have to just give up."
- "I don't know how other moms seem to have so much time because I just don't."
- "I'm just so busy."
- "I have so much to do."

One thousand, four hundred and forty minutes. That is how many minutes are in a single day. We all get them. How we use them, though, that is where so many of us go wrong.

Have you ever stared at yourself in the mirror at the end of your day, brushing your teeth, thinking, "What did I do all day? Did I get anything done at all?" Sure, we all have. As busy working moms, the days can get away from us if we don't have a strong handle on our time-management.

The highest performing moms know how to best use their time and can often get more done in a day than others do in a week. This is said as a bit of a cliché, but I believe it to be absolutely true. I am confident that some of us are far better with our time than others. I believe it is one of the key differentiators between the moms that are winning and the moms that are struggling. In this chapter, we will talk about simple and effective time-management tricks that you can use right away. These are skills that can be learned and are not magic.

If you are struggling with getting tasks done at home or at work, any one of these tips can help you be more efficient and productive. However, if you are really struggling, *do not try them all*. Trying to go from hot mess to time-management master is something that takes time. Rome was not built in a day, and an overwhelmed mom does not become a cool, calm owner of her time in a day either.

PLAN TO PLAN

First things first, you must use a calendar, planner, or scheduling app. Seriously. One of the biggest questions

I ask moms that are struggling is "Are you writing things down in a planner?"

"I have one, but I just can't get in the habit of writing in it."

"Going through it seems like such a waste of time."

"I have it all in my head."

No.

No. No. No.

If you are not writing it down—or typing it into a digital calendar or app—it is not going to happen. Have you heard the saying that failing to plan is planning to fail? It applies 100% to this situation.

If you are not planning your time, you will *never* have a good handle on it. This is the first step. It is a non-negotiable.

For me, planning happens each morning. It is part of my morning routine, and something I do every day, including weekends. You will remember we talked about morning routines previously as one of the key secrets of supermoms.

You don't have to plan in the morning. You could plan your day the night before to prepare for a fast start to your morning. You could sit down on Sunday and plan your entire week.

The point is that when you wake up on any given day and have no idea what is ahead of you, you are already in a time deficit. You are in a perfect position to lose time, waste time, and end the day wondering what the heck happened. When you plan, and actually honor your calendar, you are in charge of your time.

Using a calendar or planner also allows you to prevent double-booking. When Jeremy was traveling every week, all week, I was responsible for all of the kids' activities. We wanted them to get to play sports, do activities, and stay active despite him being gone all week. If I did not carefully plan their activities, I could never have been in two or three places at once. My planner was critical to staying on top of all of the interlaced schedules in our family.

> "
>
> STOP CLOGGING UP YOUR MEMORY WITH UNNECESSARY DETAILS THAT CAN EASILY BE PUT TO PAPER FOR SAFEKEEPING.
>
> "

Finally, your planner or calendar allows you to remember everything. Have you ever received a call from the dentist asking if you were still planning on making your appointment? Whoops.

You are busy. You are juggling a lot of balls. Keeping everything in your head is a sure way to miss appointments, forget important deadlines, and skip responsibilities.

Write. It. Down.

Getting tasks and requirements out of your head and onto paper gives your mind more space for other important thoughts like creativity and problem-solving. These abilities are vital for a happy and productive mind. Stop clogging up your memory with unnecessary details that can easily be put to paper for safekeeping.

DAY, WEEK, MONTH, QUARTER, YEAR: GOAL SETTING

What are your goals? Are you working toward a promotion? Do you want to potty train your three-year-old? Are you saving for a family vacation to the Caribbean? Do you want to get an advanced degree, attend every softball game, or learn to knit? Do you want to start a business, grow a side hustle, write a book?

Supermoms have big goals and big dreams. They think big. They think wild. They want it all. They want to be amazing in their careers and amazing moms, all at the same time.

How will you get there? How will you know if you have made it? How will you know what to make a priority?

In the previous chapter, we reviewed how to set priorities. Still, how can you know what to prioritize if you don't know your goals, if you don't know what you want?

I like the idea of setting goals based on time buckets. If I know my big goal for the year, I can work backwards all the way to know what is most important for me to do *today*.

BIG GOAL FOR THE YEAR

WHAT DO I NEED TO DO IN THE NEXT THREE MONTHS, SIX MONTHS, AND NINE MONTHS TO MAKE IT HAPPEN?

WHAT DO I NEED TO DO THIS MONTH TO MAKE IT HAPPEN?

WHAT DO I NEED TO DO THIS WEEK TO MAKE IT HAPPEN?

WHAT DO I NEED TO DO TODAY TO MAKE IT HAPPEN?

Here is an example:

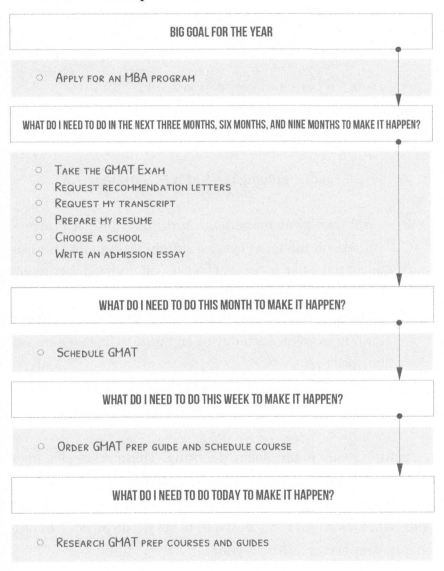

BIG GOAL FOR THE YEAR

○ APPLY FOR AN MBA PROGRAM

WHAT DO I NEED TO DO IN THE NEXT THREE MONTHS, SIX MONTHS, AND NINE MONTHS TO MAKE IT HAPPEN?

○ TAKE THE GMAT EXAM
○ REQUEST RECOMMENDATION LETTERS
○ REQUEST MY TRANSCRIPT
○ PREPARE MY RESUME
○ CHOOSE A SCHOOL
○ WRITE AN ADMISSION ESSAY

WHAT DO I NEED TO DO THIS MONTH TO MAKE IT HAPPEN?

○ SCHEDULE GMAT

WHAT DO I NEED TO DO THIS WEEK TO MAKE IT HAPPEN?

○ ORDER GMAT PREP GUIDE AND SCHEDULE COURSE

WHAT DO I NEED TO DO TODAY TO MAKE IT HAPPEN?

○ RESEARCH GMAT PREP COURSES AND GUIDES

Once you know your big goals, how will you measure them? An incredibly popular way to set and measure goals is the

S.M.A.R.T strategy. S.M.A.R.T. stands for specific, measurable, attainable, relevant, and time-based.

Here are some examples that are not S.M.A.R.T. goals:

- I want to potty train my two-year-old.
- I want to get a new job.
- I want to write a book.

Let's try it again, applying the S.M.A.R.T. strategy:

- I will take away diapers on April third and sit Princess Pamela on the toilet every thirty minutes in an effort to potty-train her in a weekend. I will know she is ready when she has one accident or less per day.
- On February first, I will update my resume. I will apply for one new job each day in an effort to have a new job by April first.
- Starting tomorrow, I will write five-hundred words per day in order to finish my novel in six months.

Setting goals might seem daunting. These strategies take some time to implement. If you want to reach your goals and not waste considerable time in the end, planning your goals and your path for success is the best way to get what you want in life, both in your career and with your family.

THE GLORIOUS TO-DO LIST

To-do lists are my number one way to stay organized and fo-cused. When your checklist is rolling around in your brain, it takes a lot of mental energy to keep it top of mind. You will 1) forget the task because there are too many thoughts for your memory to maintain, or 2) use significant mental energy not to forget and limit the amount of focus you can give to other activities.

Have you ever felt like you had so many things to do that you couldn't focus? The reason this happens is that there are too many thoughts spinning around in your head. If you put them to paper, you can get them out of your head, clear your mind, and free up mental space to organize and act.

Brain dumps are my favorite way to extract all my poten-tial to-dos. A brain dump is putting everything in your mind on paper. It allows you to get everything out of your head and look at it realistically. It allows you to prevent that swirling feeling that can come when you have too many things to do and don't know where to start.

I like to create multiple to-do lists to ensure I can dedicate appropriate time. It also keeps me from being completely overwhelmed with 110 things on one giant list. My categories are as follows:

1. Work To-Dos
2. Home To-Dos (This Week)
3. Home To-Dos (Non-Critical, Future)

I might have things like repaint the kid's bathroom, clean out the garage, and clean all the grout lines in the downstairs tile on my non-critical home list. (These are all *actually* on my current list.) These are things I don't want to forget to do, but I also don't want to spend mental energy on them until I am ready to get to them. They stay on this ongoing list that I tick off slowly as I have time.

The home to-do list for critical items is for tasks that I will actually be scheduling that week. Meal planning and grocery shopping, making necessary doctor's appointments, washing our towels, and buying birthday presents are all examples of tasks that I put on the list for this week.

Finally, I always keep work to-dos separate because I bucket my time. When I am not traveling, I work out of a home office. With an office inside my home, it would be very easy to mix tasks between home and work. If I keep a list of work tasks separate, I can use work time to only schedule work-related activities.

GIVE YOUR TIME A JOB

One of the greatest tactics to use in planning out your day is assigning time to everything. Give your time a job. Do you have to feed your baby lunch and you know that will take a good forty-five minutes with the giant mess she makes. Schedule it. Do you have to help the kids with homework? Schedule it. Do you make dinner or clean up? Schedule it.

You should not only be putting work tasks and appointments in your planner when you schedule your day. You should be determining where you will take downtime, eat, and rest.

What will your morning look like? Will you take a lunch break or work through and eat at your desk? Do you need a thirty-minute show after the kids go to bed? Make sure to put it in the schedule.

Some of you have argued that scheduling time is too rigid for you. You like to be flexible. Be honest, how is that working for you? Are you reaching your goals?

Be very careful with how you schedule your time. You may have heard of Parkinson's law. Parkinson's law was first discussed by Cyril Parkinson in a 1955 essay regarding bureaucracy and later included in his book *Parkinson's Law: The Pursuit of Progress*.[48] It is now thought to mean that tasks will take the amount of time you give them. If you give yourself one hour to finish your report, it will take you one hour. If you give yourself three hours, it will take three.

This concept works with teams and kids as well. Give your team one hour to brainstorm a solution and create a presentation, they will get it done in an hour. Give them a week and you won't have that presentation for seven days. In our house, we challenge the family to clean the entire house in twenty minutes. We set a timer, and you would be surprised how quickly a house ransacked by six humans and two giant dogs can get cleaned up.

Using this law also requires you to understand the tasks on your schedule. You might easily know how long it takes you to drive to soccer practice or empty the dishwasher or send your weekly update to your team. However, new tasks or challenging work may need a little more flexibility.

In the next section, we talk about time-wasters and task tracking that can help with knowing how long things really take you each day.

STOP TERRIBLE TIME-WASTERS

There are days when I am a bit of a time-management stickler. I loathe anything that wastes my time. Other days, I let time-wasters get the best of me. What are time-wasters?

TABLE OF TERRIBLE TIME-WASTERS				
Task Jumping	Procrastination	Saying Yes to Everything	Lack of Routine	Twitter
Starting Without Finishing	Television	Being Disorganized	Perfection	Snacking
Unnecessary Meetings	Not Having a Plan	Lack of Priorities	Facebook	Writing Checks
A Too-Long To-Do List	Inefficiency	★	Coffee Breaks	Never-ending Research
Constant Email Checking	Traffic	Netflix	Lack of Habits	Interruptions
Complaining	Multitasking	Alcohol	Instant Messenger Apps	Happy Hour
LinkedIn	Clutter	Waiting in Line	Instagram	Unnecessary Tasks

The table above includes many activities that might be an important or expected part of our day. *Netflix isn't a time-waster*, you protest, *it is my me-time at the end of a hard day!*

The point is that anything in the table above, and so many other things, can be unexpected and unwanted time drains. Our goal isn't to avoid them entirely. Instead, the goal is to manage them the best we can so they don't eat into our valuable time. We need to learn to plan for them and expect them, if possible.

Let's start with procrastination, never-ending research, and perfection. These are different methods to get to the same end. You never get the task done.

But, I need to make sure it is perfect! But, I can't finish a project that hasn't been fully vetted.

I need you to understand that nothing is permanent.

Let's say you are painting your bedroom. You have looked at every image on Pinterest in your desired color of a nice light grey. You have researched the best paint and primer combinations. You have purchased twenty-seven different test samples from your local hardware store. You have polled no less than sixteen friends to ask their favorite color choice. You searched "best room painting strategies" and "best paint rollers for inside walls." You have spent countless hours, leaving no stone unturned to ensure the perfect result.

Your room is still not painted. The goal, the painted room, is not done because of procrastination, never-ending research, and the need for perfection.

Paint the wall. Nothing is permanent. Paint the wall. Hate it? Repaint.

There are activities on our time-waster list that cannot be avoided. You can't get out of waiting in traffic, waiting in line at the store, or paying bills. These are the time-wasters to be managed instead of avoided altogether.

Can you take public transportation or a cab and use the time in traffic to your advantage? Can you use the time to listen to a required training, an audiobook, or a podcast? Can you set up auto-pay for your bills so you don't spend extra time paying them as well as tracking your finances?

There are also things in our table that we actually *like*. Maybe we like them a lot. Happy hour, Facebook, coffee breaks, television, and instant messenger apps all can bring us some level of joy. The problem is that they are very easy to get out of control. Your ten-minute Facebook scroll to see your friends' kids can turn into a forty-five-minute rabbit hole of political posts, silly memes, and taking the latest quiz to see which Disney princess you are today.

This is not time well spent. You will know this especially because, at the end of your forty-five-minute scroll, you will likely not feel refreshed. Instead, you may feel frustrated that you just wasted forty-five minutes and barely realized it. You might feel guilty. You might feel angry or annoyed, especially if you spent time looking at posts and photos that you don't especially like.

We have to value our time and the responsibilities we put in it.

You might be thinking, "I don't even know what all my time-wasters are yet!" The best way to see where your time is going is to track it. Task tracking is documenting your time in fifteen-minute blocks. Every fifteen minutes, you write down what you did for the last fifteen minutes. Don't make any changes, just note everything you do for a few days in a row. You will quickly see where time is being well spent and where hours and minutes are slipping away. The goal is not to control your time but to just be aware of how long tasks are taking. It can be tedious but does help you get a handle on where your time is going each day so you can better manage it into the future.

EAT THAT FROG

We started this chapter with a quote attributed to Mark Twain. Twain said, "If it's your job to eat a frog, it's best to do it first thing in the morning. And if it's your job to eat two frogs, it's best to eat the biggest one first." I sincerely hope it is not your job to eat frogs.

Twain's point is that if you have to do a hard thing, if you have a hard task on your plate for the day, it is best to just get it done. Do it first. If you have two hard tasks, do the hardest first, then do the next hardest.

If you tend to procrastinate, this is a perfect strategy. If your day tends to get away from you, this is again a perfect strategy. You don't give yourself time to think about it, and just do the thing.

Envision you are at work early and you have a long list of actions for your day. Email, meetings, budget reviews, sales calls, and the list goes on. Should you start your day with email? Not only does starting your day with email, likely one of the easier things on your list, waste precious brainpower early in the day, it also derails your day, especially if you have emails that require your action.

Instead, start your day with the most difficult task. Let's say you have a complicated budget review due by 3:00 p.m. Starting your day with the hardest task allows you to win the day. The hardest thing is already done, so even if the rest of the day is completely derailed, you completed the most critical task on your list.

WHEN NOT TO EAT THE FROG

I will caveat the idea of "eating the frog" with one thing. Sometimes the idea of doing the hardest thing first feels completely overwhelming. Maybe your to-do list is so long that you don't even know what is the hardest and what is the biggest priority. You start spinning, panicking, and don't know where to start.

This is not productive use of time. It also leads to increased stress and burn out. Remember, when struggling with motivation, the best thing to do is...*just...start.*

Pick something easy and do it. Then, pick something else easy and do that. A mom in motion stays in motion. Once you get traction, momentum on checking things off your list, you are more likely to keep that momentum going to get things done.

———————————

SUPERMOM SHORTCUT • THE SECRET OF TIME MANAGEMENT • CHAPTER WRAP UP

WHAT WE LEARNED

Managing your time is critical to your success as a busy working mom. Without tools in place to track, document, and assign your time, you are likely to fall prey to the terrible time-wasters that try to throw us off track.

HOW WE APPLY IT

Getting a handle on your time can be *tough*. Here are the actionable steps from this chapter to get more from your 1,440 minutes each day.

- Use a planner, calendar, or scheduling app on your phone and use it to plan all of your time.
- Set important goals for the day, week, month, quarter, and year.
- Consistently use to-do lists to avoid missed activities or tasks.
- Give your time a job and stick to it.
- Stop wasting time or letting time get away from you.
- Do the hardest thing on your list first to win the day.
- Start with easy tasks to get motivation started when you are feeling overwhelmed.

ONE SMALL STEP

Brain dump your to-do list. Write down everything you need to do for work and home. Then, use one of the strategies from this chapter to split up those tasks and get to it.

WHAT COMES NEXT

Now that we know how to prioritize the most important things and manage our time, it is time to get productive. Chapter 14 tells how supermoms work smarter, not harder.

CHAPTER 14
SUPERMOMS WORK SMARTER, NOT HARDER

THE SECRET OF PRODUCTIVITY

"If you want something done, ask a busy person."

— Proverb, Anonymous

"Focus on being productive instead of busy."

— Tim Ferriss, *The 4-Hour Workweek: Escape 9–5, Live Anywhere, and Join the New Rich*[49]

"Productivity is never an accident. It is always the result of a commitment to excellence, intelligent planning and focused effort."

— Paul J. Meyer[50]

"**D**o you think you could just host the baby shower?" her mom asked.

"Um…I guess," she responded slowly with apprehension.

Her mom went on, "You know how they always say to ask a busy person if you want something done. I just figure you always find a way to make things happen, so you are the perfect person for the job."

Jennifer was the oldest of three sisters, the only one with a career, and had five kids. Her sisters each had one child and spent their days at mom groups and play centers. She was undoubtedly the one with the least available time on her hands. Planning a baby shower for their cousin was not something she wanted to add to her plate.

"Mom, don't you think Cindi or Randi would rather host?" she asked, hopeful this might lead her mom in the direction of her sisters.

"You know how overwhelmed they get with the babies. I think you would just do a better job."

Well, thanks, Mom. Cue eyeroll. Jennifer said yes—and the baby shower was amazing, of course.

The point of this story about my friend—who may be a bit of a pushover—was not that you should say yes to things you don't have time to do. It isn't that you should be a sucker or fill up every moment of your time. It isn't even that you should let your mom manipulate you with veiled compliments.

The point is that, busy as she was, she was able to squeeze in a hosted party because her productivity skills were seriously on point. She found she always had available time to squeeze in last-minute bake sale requests, volunteer hours, or client meetings.

She works smarter with her time so she can work harder only when she wants. She is seriously amazing.

Time management and productivity go hand in hand, but they are not the same. Time management is understanding your time. It is giving your time a job and making sure every necessary task has place on your schedule so it isn't missed or forgotten.

Productivity is using that time to the best of your ability. It is being efficient. It is focusing on getting the important things done on the task at hand, not just on being busy and having all of your time full. It is about focusing on needle movers in your home or business.

Supermoms are said to get more done in a day than others do in a week. Again, I believe this to be the literal truth. This chapter is filled with what I like to call "productivity hacks." Small changes in how you currently do things can make a huge difference in how much you actually get done.

Can you imagine being so productive that you had an extra three hours a week of free time? What would you do? Lunch date with your partner? Pedicure and a massage? Take an extra Pilates class? Play with your kids at the park without distraction? A roaring game of Monopoly? Take a nap?

We all want more time in our day. The better we can use the time we have to be efficient and productive, the more flexibility in our day and our life.

USE EVERY SMALL MOMENT

I am going to start with one of my favorite productivity hacks. Make use of super small pockets of time. You know those ten minutes waiting in the school pick-up line, the fifteen-minute drive to soccer practice, or five minutes waiting for dance class to let out. I love these tiny pockets of time.

What do you do during this time? If I had to guess, I bet you scroll your phone. You check Facebook, you look at Instagram, you watch adorable cat videos.

What if you had a list of items that only take five or ten minutes? During this time, you could:

- Schedule doctors' appointments
- Respond to quick but necessary emails
- Call a client
- Do a five-minute meditation to prepare for the rest of your evening
- Listen to a few minutes of an audiobook on productivity
- Make your meal plan for the week
- Create a grocery list
- Voice record an entire blog post or meeting agenda
- Read a report or brief
- Create a plan for your next day
- Call your dad

Productive supermoms know they need to use every bit of available time. They realize how much of this "in-between time" gets wasted in a day, a week, a month. Every single one of these tasks can be done quickly but still eats into your day. When you plan to use those small pockets of time, you can save hours per week.

KNOW YOUR ENERGY FLOW

Another important productivity hack of mine is to know your energy flow. You have to know when your energy is at its best and when it is low throughout your day. For me, and for many high-performing moms, I am a powerhouse early in the morning. I own the world at 4:00 a.m. I am energized, and my brain is on fire first thing.

Although a lot of people are higher energy in the morning after sleep—"larks"—others may be referred to as "owls," as in night owls. They are higher energy and have higher productivity in the nighttime hours. Some women are somewhere in between.

If you are not sure where you have the most energy, track it. Spend a few days noting when you feel high energy and when you feel a slump. Note what things seem to increase your energy and what seems to deplete it.

Once you know your high-energy times, use that to determine how you allocate your time in your schedule. For example, I am never going to write chapters of my book or a thoughtful blog post in the middle of the afternoon. I am never going to do an intense review of a contract right after dinner. These things, for me, are morning tasks when my energy is highest and mental capacity is best.

I am going to schedule tasks like perfunctory email, expense report reviews, and folding laundry for after meals when my energy is low and motivation is waning.

DONE IS BETTER THAN PERFECT

Productivity masters know one thing. Procrastination and perfection are enemies of productivity. Done is always better than perfect. In-progress is always better than not started.

Supermoms don't wait for the perfect moment to start a side hustle. They just do it. They don't wait for the client to notice something is missing. They just fix it. They don't wait to feel ready for a promotion. They jump in feet first and learn to swim.

Think about how often you spend time trying to do something perfectly. Word the perfect email that will get the point across but won't make anyone angry. Write the perfect report. Make a perfectly plated dinner. Help your preteen design the perfect science project.

Perfection is for surgeons, not for writing emails.

The need to be perfect and to procrastinate every task wastes time. It eliminates efficiency. The saddest part is that, most of the time, it doesn't matter. The client doesn't care if you used the word necessary or obligatory. The kids don't care if the socks are folded inside out or folded at all.

Almost everything can be changed. Almost everything can be tweaked. If you finish the task and it got the job done, great. If you finished and it missed the mark, again, in-progress is always better than not started at all.

TASK BATCH

If you have similar tasks that need to be done, put those like tasks together. When you are in the same mindset, it is easier to move between tasks than it is to switch from one completely different task to another. Going from making dinner to assessing a client budget to meeting with your child's coach to sewing a costume for the school play is much harder than putting tasks requiring similar skills or similar locations together.

Do you need to sew costumes and also have a few buttons to sew on your suit jackets? Do those together.

Do you need to compare financial reports, approve expense reports, and reconcile QuickBooks? Do those together.

When my babies were still in carrier car seats, I would pick one day or one afternoon to do all of my errands. We would leave the house and get in and out of the hot car six or seven times. Summer in Phoenix can be 115 degrees or more, so errands were never fun with an infant. Instead of spreading that out over a week, I would batch them all together so we only had to get through it once.

Unclick the carrier, unbuckle the toddler, rush through all the stores in that stop. Click, buckle, unclick, unbuckle.

Oil change. Check. Return cute, but too tight, wedges to Target and simultaneously pick up a birthday gift for my sister. Check. Bank withdrawal. Check. Pick up supplies for our Halloween costumes at the craft supply store. Check. Gas at the gas station. Check. Grocery shopping. Check.

Going out once and being "in the zone" to get those jobs done made them far more efficient than going out repeatedly all week long.

TIME BLOCK

Most people cannot do the same activity for more than about fifty to ninety minutes without becoming fatigued. Fatigue means you will not do the task as well or as fast. Think of an all-day meeting with no breaks? Would you be at the top of your game by the end of the day? Of course not.

The essence of time blocking is that you create a block of time for a specific task, no disruptions. You work only on that task and then you take a break.

Multitasking—which is actually jumping quickly from task to task and not "multitasking" at all—is not productive. It is not efficient, and it is not an effective way to schedule your time. The power of time blocking is that you are focused on one specific task. You are honed in on getting this assignment done well before taking a break or moving to another task.

A question I get a lot is, "What happens if I have a big project to complete? I can't just block time to do the whole thing. It takes me way too long."

Never block your time for more than about an hour at a time without a planned break. Breaks and rest, with some great options discussed in Chapter 10, are critical to maintaining energy and brainpower.

These blocks of time are also, ideally, distraction free. Those of us with lots of tiny humans living with us understand that distractions are the name of the game. Naptime, babysitter time, daycare time, school time, and trading with your partner are all great ways to limit those distractions called children.

Are you thinking you don't have any of those options? May I recommend Chapter 4 on The Secret of Help?

USE YOUR PHONE TO WIN

Cell phones can be the enemy. In this book, we have talked about how things like unexpected phone calls, emails, and social media can be energy drains and time sucks. They can get in the way of being as efficient as possible. They can certainly be terrible time-wasters.

You can also use your phone to win the day by using reminders. I have three favorite ways of using phone reminders:

1. Set a reminder for your arrival at a certain place. For example, you can set a reminder to go off every time you get to your house or the grocery store or baseball practice. If you want to get better at being productive during baseball practice, you could set a reminder that says "Time to GET THINGS DONE" every time you get to the ball field. You will be surprised at how powerful these little reminders can be to keep you on track.

2. My second favorite way to use my phone to remind me of my goals is by setting alarms. When I was writing this very book, I had an alarm set in my phone to go off at 2:45 p.m. every day. It said, "You are an author! You will change lives!" I never remembered this alarm was going to go off, and it was a solid reminder of my biggest goal every single day.

3. A final way to use your phone for staying strong and efficient I learned from Brendon Burchard on his podcast, The Brendon

Show[51]. He recommends setting alarms in your phone with three words reminding you who you want to be. For example, I have three alarms set at various times throughout the day. They read:

HAPPY | CALM | HEALTHY
SUPPORTIVE | POSITIVE | ENTHUSIASTIC
ENERGIZED | PATIENT | SUPERMOM

Again, I never remember these are going to go off, but they remind me that I need to be my best. They remind me especially when I am *not* being my best.

You will start to find your phone reminding you at just the right moment when you get these alarms right.

YOU MUST BE ORGANIZED

I know, I know. This one is annoying. For those of you that like everything in its place, you love this idea. Those of you that like a little bit of a mess, stay with me.

If you want to be productive, you need to be able to find things easily. They need to be in the proximity of your project. If it takes you seven minutes to find your car keys before you head out the door to run your errands, those are seven minutes wasted. If it takes you ten minutes of digging through your desktop to find the report you were working to finish today, those are ten more minutes wasted.

You don't have to be Martha Stewart, but you do need to have some method to your madness. If you can't find the broom, it's tough to sweep the floor.

KNOW WHAT'S WORKING

How will you know if any of your productivity changes are actually working? How will you know if you are getting things done faster or with higher quality?

Here is where daily or weekly reviews come into play. I like to review my week on Sundays. Each Sunday, I look at what has happened over the last week. Did I meet all my goals? Were there things I missed or places I went wrong? Did I feel happy with my results or was I stressed and burned out?

I also look forward at my next week and decide if anything needs to change. Do I need to shift tasks? Did I give myself enough time for every work activity, every home activity and time to rest? Do I need help?

> YOU BECOME A BETTER MOM, A BETTER WIFE, A BETTER COACH, A BETTER EMPLOYEE, A BETTER BOSS. YOU BECOME BETTER.

When you get into the habit of doing this every single week, you get better at managing your time. You get better at knowing how long recurring tasks take. You get better at paying attention to how you feel.

You become a better mom, a better wife, a better coach, a better employee, a better boss. You become better.

WHAT WE LEARNED

Time management and productivity go hand in hand. If you don't have a handle on your time, you can't be productive with it. Productivity is getting things done efficiently and focusing on the most important things, not just filling your time.

HOW WE APPLY IT

Small changes to the way you spend your day or your week can greatly impact your productivity. Some strategies we talk about in this chapter are:

- Use Every Small Moment: Small moments throughout your day can be wasted if you are not strategic about them.
- Know Your Energy Flow: Everyone has a time of day when they have the most energy and a time when their energy dips. Use this to your advantage.
- Done Is Better Than Perfect: Done is always better than perfect. There is nothing that can't be changed, fixed, or tweaked. Nothing is permanent.
- Task Batch: Find like activities and do them together, whether in the same topic area, in the same space, or needing the same supplies.
- Time Block: Assign blocks of time to your tasks, use this time without distraction and always make sure you take breaks.

- Use Your Phone to Win: Use your phone to set reminders and alarms to keep you on track both in mindset and with regard to time.
- You Must Be Organized: If you can't find the tools to complete your task, you can't be productive.
- Know What Is Working: Weekly evaluations allow you to know what is working, make changes, and stay aware of your emotional and physical impact.

ONE SMALL STEP

Set reminders or alarms in your phone for who you want to be or how you want to act.

Do you want to remind yourself that you can grocery shop in 30 minutes or less? Set a reminder to ring every time you arrive at the store that says, "You are a fast shopper and don't buy junk."

Do you want to be calm and focused on your family when you get home each night? Set a reminder to go off every time you return home that says, "You are calm. You are family-focused. You are supermom."

WHAT COMES NEXT

In the next chapter, we review problem-solving strategies. When you allow "the culture of complaint" to infiltrate work or home, you lose control of your team. Learning to manage and solve problems keeps complaining to a minimum and happiness high.

CHAPTER 15
SUPERMOMS DON'T TOLERATE A "CULTURE OF COMPLAINT"

THE SECRET OF PROBLEM-SOLVING

"So you watch yourself about complaining, Sister. What you're supposed to do when you don't like a thing is change it. If you can't change it, change the way you think about it. Don't complain."

— Maya Angelou, *Wouldn't Take Nothing for My Journey Now*[52]

"If you took one-tenth the energy you put into complaining and applied it to solving the problem, you'd be surprised by how well things can work out... Complaining does not work as a strategy. We all have finite time and energy. Any time we spend whining is unlikely to help us achieve our goals. And it won't make us happier."

— Randy Pausch, *The Last Lecture*[53]

I got in the back of the black Chevy Suburban, the sixth mom on the pick-up route. Stacy drove around the neighborhood to pick up some of the moms for our long-overdue dinner date. I was the last to be picked up, greeted the other moms, and was ready to dive into a great night of relaxing conversation and much-needed friend time.

The complaining had already started. Complaining about husbands and kids and work and the carpool lane. Complaining about homework and deadlines and dirty houses and exhaustion.

The displeasure with nearly all things in their lives continued for most of the dinner and the ride home.

Despite being an extrovert to the max, this night left me drained, tired, and feeling more negatively about my own life than I did when the night started.

Wasn't a mom date supposed to be fun? Wasn't it supposed to be refreshing and bring a little jolt of joy to my soul?

THE CULTURE OF COMPLAINT

While I have used this term frequently in my career, I never really applied it to my friend time or my home time. That night was a realization!

What exactly is the "culture of complaint"? The culture of complaint is when we set up an atmosphere, a culture, where complaining is tolerated at best and encouraged at worst.

I have often used this in the work setting to describe teams that have, usually unintentionally, allowed their team meetings, their emails, and their overall communication to permit a large amount of complaining. Let me be clear, this is not the same as identifying a problem. This is not the same as conflict-resolution. Complaining is more like whining with no intention of providing a solution.

"This client is always asking for more and more and more. I hate working with them."

"Julia is always finding things wrong with my reports. I bet she never does that to anyone else."

"Why do we always have to be the ones to clean up the break-room?"

When we allow or encourage our colleagues to complain, we unconsciously start to identify areas where we ourselves may be disgruntled.

"Yeah, why *do* we always have to clean up the breakroom? No one else ever does it."

Instead of cultivating a culture of conflict-resolution, a culture of problem-solving, we cultivate a culture where we let the team bring each other down. Brick by brick, we start to eat away at team comradery, performance, and overall happiness at work.

And it is the same with friends and at home.

When we encourage a culture of complaint, we encourage friends or loved ones to find the areas of their life where they are unhappy—and not in a constructive, self-help sort of way, not even in a "venting" sort of way. This culture is destructive and can bring down whole families and teams.

Let me help make this concept clear with a few examples:

	CULTURE OF COMPLAINT	VENTING	PROBLEM-SOLVING
WHAT IS IT?	○ Complaining without intent to solve a problem ○ Whining ○ Encouraging others to complain along with you, often done without intention ○ Nit-picking ○ Often stated with the words "always" or "never"	○ Voicing emotional frustration over a situation in advance of the problem-solving stage ○ Note: Venting can look a lot like complaining. The difference is that the venter is intentionally releasing the emotions from the situation before working on a rational solution	○ Identifying an unhappy situation and subsequently finding one or more solutions to the problem ○ Conflict/resolution where we first identify the conflict and then identify one or more ways to resolve the issue
AT WORK	○ Our boss always makes the dumbest decisions. He is probably the stupidest one in the c-suite. ○ I always get asked to do the crappy jobs. I never get any of the cool tasks.	○ Ugh! I am so frustrated with this team. They are all arguing and nothing is getting done!!! Ok, let's think about a team-building activity. I think everyone is overworked and no one feels appreciated or heard.	○ Marcy, I really feel like the team is frustrated. Can we sit down and go through each task so they understand the end goal? ○ I am feeling overwhelmed with all the tasks this week. Can we talk about the order of priority?

	CULTURE OF COMPLAINT	VENTING	PROBLEM-SOLVING
WITH FRIENDS	○ JIM IS ALWAYS LEAVING EARLY FOR MEETINGS, AND HE NEVER HELPS ME WITH ANYTHING. ○ CINDY IS SO NEEDY. I AM ALWAYS HAVING TO TALK HER OFF A LEDGE, BUT SHE NEVER LISTENS TO ME AT ALL.	○ I AM ABOUT TO LOSE MY MIND! AHHH! I CAN'T HANDLE ALL THE COMPLAINING AT OUR MOMS' NIGHT OUT. MAYBE AT THE NEXT NIGHT OUT, I CAN MAKE A PLAN TO ASK EVERYONE ABOUT THE BEST THING THEY DID THAT WEEK TO SET IT OFF ON A POSITIVE NOTE.	○ JILL, I FEEL LIKE I AM DROWNING AND WONDERING IF YOU COULD TRADE CHILDCARE WITH ME THIS WEEK? I'LL TAKE YOUR KIDS FOR A FEW HOURS ON SATURDAY IF YOU TAKE MINE ON SUNDAY? ○ BONNIE, I FEEL LIKE YOU ARE ANNOYED WITH ME. DO YOU WANT TO TALK ABOUT IT?
AT HOME	○ YOU KIDS NEVER DO ANYTHING I ASK YOU TO DO. ○ I AM ALWAYS THE ONE TO MAKE DINNER PLANS AND NO ONE EVER HELPS ME.	○ IF I HAVE TO ASK ONE MORE CHILD TO PICK UP THEIR SHOES, I AM GOING TO SCREAM! AHHH! OK, I AM GOING TO GET A SHOE BASKET AND PUT IT RIGHT BY THE FRONT DOOR. IF IT IS EASY TO PUT THEIR SHOES AWAY, MAYBE THEY WILL DO IT MORE OFTEN.	○ MOMMY IS FEELING REALLY FRUSTRA- TED WITH ALL THE HOUSE CHORES. WE ARE GOING TO SET A TIMER, PUT ON SUPERHERO CAPES, BLAST THE MUSIC, AND SEE HOW MUCH WE CAN GET DONE IN TWENTY MINUTES. READY, SET, GO!

Not only does simple complaining bring down your mood, your attitude, and your energy, it also starts the "blame game." As you can see in our examples, complaining nearly always is directed at someone else. The complainer makes things the boss's fault, Jim's fault, or the kids' fault.

When we allow a culture of complaint, we encourage people to look for the worst *and* blame it on others. This is certainly not the place I want to work. It isn't the place I want to live.

What can complaining or blame actually do to you besides making you feel like crap?

- It increases cortisol, one of the stress hormones, which has been linked to increased blood pressure, increased blood sugar, impairs your immune system, and causes you to be more susceptible to high cholesterol, diabetes, heart disease, and obesity.[54] Basically, it makes you sick.
- Complaining cultivates a negative attitude, allowing you to look for the worst in a situation instead of looking for the positive.
- Blame while complaining puts the situation in someone else's control, causing the complainer to feel powerless over the situation.
- Complaining can rewire the brain by shrinking the hippocampus. The hippocampus is responsible for cognitive ability and memory. When you complain consistently, the brain reduces memory capacity as well as the ability to react in new situations.
- Negative thoughts breed more negative thoughts.

A PROBLEM-SOLVING MINDSET

It is *so easy* to complain, especially when you have continually encouraged the habit. What can you do to encourage a problem-solving mindset in yourself, your team, or your home? How do you change your brain to start thinking about a solution instead of only reacting to the emotion that the problem is causing?

IDENTIFY THE THOUGHT BEHIND THE EMOTION

Complaining is always based in emotion. You feel overwhelmed at the amount of work you have to complete. You feel frustrated that your partner doesn't help you more often or more consistently. You feel irritated that the kids keep leaving bowls on the table.

Identifying the thought means sitting with the emotion and looking for the thought behind it without judgement. You will identify the thoughts even if they might be irrational.

I am frustrated that I did not get the promotion. My thoughts include:

- My vice president does not trust me.
- My boss does not think I am competent.
- I will never get a promotion.

Once you have identified the initial thoughts, you can start to dig deeper to find the real problem.

DIGGING FOR THE ROOT

You may have heard of "root cause analysis." In simple terms, root cause analysis is asking "why" over and over until you get to the root of your problem. Here is an example:

- I am frustrated that my director doesn't give me more high-level tasks. I always get the crappy stuff to do.
- **Why does that make you frustrated?**
- The crappy stuff doesn't challenge me.
- **Why do you want to be challenged?**
- My work would be more fulfilling for me if I was challenged.
- **Why is it important for your work to be fulfilling?**
- I would feel happier and more competent. I would know that my director believed I was competent.

As we continue to ask "why," we get from the assumed problem of "I always get the crappy stuff to do" to the real problem. The real problem is that I don't feel competent, and I don't think my director believes I am competent.

If we don't dig deep to find the root cause, we may try to solve the wrong problem.

THINK SOLUTION, NOT PROBLEM

We have identified our emotion and the true problem. It is now time to focus on the solution. Corporate researchers have found that a solution-focused strategy, where focus is on enhancing the solution and finding things that are already going well, may work better, especially in dysfunctional teams, than a problem-focused approach[55] A problem-focused approach focuses on what is going wrong and focuses on what one doesn't want instead of what one does want.

If you focus on what you want to happen instead of what you don't want to happen, you are better able to find the right solution.

> IF YOU FOCUS ON WHAT YOU WANT TO HAPPEN INSTEAD OF WHAT YOU DON'T WANT TO HAPPEN, YOU ARE BETTER ABLE TO FIND THE RIGHT SOLUTION.

THE BIG QUESTION

Do you actually want a change?

After you identify the emotion that is happening, figure out the problem, and target a solution-focused approach, you need to make a big decision. Do you actually want a change? Often times, the answer is a resounding *yes*. I wouldn't be complaining if I didn't want a change, sheesh.

You would be surprised, though, how often you might get to this part of the problem and realize that the solution is more work that you are willing to put in. You might figure out that the problem wasn't really that big of a deal after all. You might figure out that you just like to complain and feel like a martyr but don't want the problem resolved. You might figure out that you actually can't change the situation and have to change your reaction to it instead.

If you decide that the solution is important to you, absolutely move on to the next steps. If not, you need to decide how you will come to terms with the problem so it doesn't continue to cause negative emotions in your life. Don't be a lifelong complainer.

THE SOLUTION BRAINSTORM

You have decided you want to solve the problem. Fantastic! You have decided you will focus on solutions and what you *want* to happen instead of on the problem itself. Perfect! Now, it is time to brainstorm.

Get out a piece of paper or use your Secrets of Supermom Workbook. Write down all the solutions you think will solve the problem. Don't be afraid to get creative or silly. The point is to think of every solution possible.

Problem:
The kids always leave their bowls on the table.

Solutions:

1. Yell at them every time they do it, and hope they change their behavior.
2. Don't let them eat.
3. Tell them what a great job they are doing when they put the bowls in the sink and how helpful they are, even if you have to remind them.

4. Give them a star sticker each time they remember on their own and let them use stars to buy prizes.

5. Put the bowls away yourself and feel angry each time.

6. Teach them about habit stacking and repeat "when I stand up from the table, I pick up my bowl" every time they eat, until it becomes automatic.

7. Decide that you no longer care if the table is messy.

8. Put the bowls away yourself and decide that you would rather have a clean table than a daily struggle.

You can see that there are plenty of ways to solve the problem. Some are certainly not solution-focused, and some would definitely cause other problems. The point is to think about everything you could possibly do to create a solution.

SIMPLIFY

You have brainstormed all the solutions to your problem. Now, you are going to simplify the plan. One of the secrets of supermoms is to work smarter, not harder. There is no reason that the complicated solution is the best. Most often, the easy and most straightforward answer is the one that is right.

Let's explore a problem you might have at work. Your client is frustrated because your product arrived late and sent a scathing email. You are tempted to complain about how annoying they are or how they always find something to complain about when they receive deliveries.

Instead, you decided to use the problem-solving mindset and have made a conscious decision to be solution-focused. You have brainstormed all of your ideas to make the client feel understood and fix the problem.

You have thought about a partial refund and free product. You have thought about free shipping on the next order. You have thought about dropping them as a client. You have your list. What will be your most simple, time-conscious, and cost-conscious path forward?

You will call the client directly, apologize for the error, and ask what you can do to remedy the situation. Simple, direct, and free.

DEFINE THE STEPS

Some simple solutions may have one easy step. If that is the case, move on and implement. However, some problems are far more complex, like a major problem with your team or a significant behavior issue with one of your children. One simple step may not be enough.

When that is the case, breaking down the solution into the steps it will take is helpful. Begin with the end in mind, and work backwards until you get to the best first step to take.

You can use the same goal setting strategies from Chapter 12 with the completed solution as the goal.

IMPLEMENT

Do the thing. Take the first step. Get started on the solution. It seems like this might be the hardest part. The hardest part is really getting past the emotion and changing the habit of complaint.

You have already worked out the steps, so getting started is easier than you think.

REALIZE YOUR POWER

The best part of the problem-solving mindset is that you realize your power. You are in control of your thoughts and how you react to a situation. You are in control of how you choose to think and feel. You are in control of how you decide to move forward to solve a problem.

You can't control them, but you can always control you.

PASS IT ON

The best part about perfecting problem-solving is that you can help others with these same steps. We talked early in this chapter about how a culture of complaint can really bring down teams and families. Change your own thinking to be more solution-focused, and you can support others to ask the same questions.

Think about how a conversation with your best friend might go.

Best Friend: Ugh! Todd is getting on my last nerve! He never helps with the laundry, he leaves dishes in the sink, and he thinks all the cleaning is my job. We both work full time! (You know that she will go on and on about this without any plan to fix the problem.)

You: That sounds frustrating! (You are validating her emotion.)

Best Friend: I am just irritated all the time. It is exhausting.

You: Why do you think it is so irritating to you right now? (You are helping her dig for the root cause instead of spiraling into a cycle of complaint.)

Best Friend: Well, I have a big deadline at the end of the month, so I am working like crazy and can't do everything.

You: What have you done in the past when you felt like you were doing everything? (Identifying solutions for the real problem.)

Best Friend: Todd and I had a heart to heart, and I told him how stressed I was at work. He agreed to shift the balance of some of our tasks at home until my deadline was done. (She identifies a solution that has worked in the past.)

You: Do you think that would work here? (You help her decide if this is a good first step.)

Best Friend: Probably. Yeah, I should definitely talk to him. (She is ready to implement.)

I will be honest. Sometimes conversations with your friends or your team or your children will go like this. Sometimes they won't. There will be those that really want to complain and have no intention to create a better situation. They prefer to blame others. They don't want to take responsibility.

It is hard to be around those that complain just for the sake of complaining and not be drawn in. Be careful with whom you spend your time and your energy.

SUPERMOM SHORTCUT • THE SECRET OF PROBLEM-SOLVING • CHAPTER WRAP UP

WHAT WE LEARNED

Complaining without intent to solve a problem is destructive to our attitude, our health, and to our mind. Encouraging a work or home life where complaining is the norm, "a culture of complaint," will lead to a pessimistic, tantrum-filled house or team. It will lead to people blaming each other when things go wrong instead of coming together to make work or life better.

HOW WE APPLY IT

Encourage a problem-solving mindset, first in yourself and then in your family and teams. If you have a hard time not automatically turning to complaining, break it down into the following steps:

- Identify the Thought Behind the Emotion
- Digging for the Root
- Think Solution, Not Problem
- The Big Question
- The Solution Brainstorm
- Simplify
- Define the Steps
- Implement
- Realize Your Power

ONE SMALL STEP

Identify areas in your life where you are complaining or where you are encouraging a "culture of complaint". Decide today that you will make a change to stop the negative, pessimistic atmosphere.

WHAT COMES NEXT

In our final chapter, we talk about the skill of marketing. Presenting something in its best light isn't just for sales teams. You must know how to sell to your team and your family as well.

CHAPTER 16
SUPERMOMS CAN SELL ANYTHING

THE SECRET OF MARKETING

"Sales are contingent upon the attitude of the salesman—not
the attitude of the prospect."

— W. Clement Stone

"Pretend that every single person you meet has a sign around
his or her neck that says, 'Make me feel important.' Not only
will you succeed in sales, you will succeed in life."

— Mary Kay Ash

For the last eight years, we have dressed up in family Hallow-een costumes. I am not talking about our family dressing up for trick-or-treating. The entire family dresses up in the same theme. We have done *Alice in Wonderland, Wizard of Oz,* "Our Family is a Circus," and so many more.

We started when Kami was only a baby, making Kinley newly four years old and Kaden two years old. At the age of four, Kinley firmly knew what she wanted in life. If you have ever interacted with a four-year-old, you know that they all are very independent. They know what they want.

How was I going to convince Little Miss Sassy-Pants that she did not want to be the princess of the moment and instead would be Alice from *Alice in Wonderland?* How would I make *her* want to be Alice instead of forcing her to be part of our family costume against her will?

Isn't this often the struggle at work and at home? We want someone to do something, or need them to do something. We know that if we force them, if we demand they do it, we may not get the results we want. They may do it, but they may become resentful or disgruntled. They may throw a giant fit on the office floor—I may or may not be talking about kids or employees at this point.

How can we convince them that this is what they want? How can we make them feel like this was their idea in the first place? Marketing!

You might think I am kidding here, but I have often said to my friends, "I can sell anything to my kids." I know them. I know what they like and don't like. I know how to talk to them so they feel like *they* made the choice and are even excited about it—I guess I am hoping here that they have no interest in reading my book and won't learn my tricks.

You don't have to be the head of marketing to need marketing and sales skills in the office. Everyone with any job has to sell either a product or themselves at some point—what do you think an interview is? The marketing and sales skills we learn at work can be easily used at home. The skills we learn to "sell" to our kids can be used at work. Win-win.

LISTEN AND LEARN

The number one quality of any good salesperson, any good marketer, and any good mom is listening. You have to listen to know what they want. I am not talking about "mom listening" where you are distracted with sixteen different things and only kind of catching every third word. Truly listening.

I listen when my kids tell me stories about kids from school. I listen when they detail every single moment of their video game rivalry. I listen to them tell me each moment of their bike jump, school presentation, or argument with a friend. I listen when they are mad, sad, excited, and scared. I listen.

When we listen, our clients feel important. Our kids feel important. Our team members, friends, and partners feel important. They feel like they matter.

Let's go back to my story about Kinley and the proposed Alice costume. She thought she wanted to be a princess, but what she really wanted was beautiful hair, a big, poufy dress, and fancy shoes.

So, how did I sell Alice?

I told her how amazing her long, curled hair would look with a big black bow. I showed her pictures of the big, poufy blue dress, her favorite color of the moment, and how it would be so fluffy when she spun around in it. I detailed every part of the sparkly, black shoes, only the fanciest, of course.

Boom.

TELL A GOOD STORY

Donald Miller wrote a book called *Building a StoryBrand*[56] and ultimately built it into an entire marketing company. Its tagline is "clarify your message so your customers will listen," and it focuses on taking your customer through the Hero's Journey. If you are not familiar with the Hero's Journey, in a nutshell, the main character in any story sets out on a quest, encounters problems, finds a friend to help, learns an important lesson with which is transformed, and returns victorious.

You can find the Hero's Journey in books, movies, and marketing alike. Think *Star Wars, Back to the Future, The Matrix, 10 Things I Hate About You,* and *The Breakfast Club*, just to name a few.

When you know how to tell a good story, you can bring people in. This goes for employees, clients, friends, and children. Think of someone you love talking with, either on a professional or personal level. I bet they tell good stories.

When I am talking to my kids about what we will do or where we will go, I tell them a story about it, starring them as the lead character. I tell them how, when going to the doctor, they will walk in brave, we will see how much they weigh and how smart and strong they have become. They will show the doctor all of their new and amazing skills—*maybe have a quick shot*—and then off for ice cream.

Maybe we need to run errands. Instead, I call it an adventure. I point out all the fun stops we will make, downplaying the ones they will find annoying.

Telling a good story, with your client or child as the lead, will help them see themselves where you want them to be, whether that is behind the wheel of that new car or in the line for flu shots.

HANDLING OBJECTIONS

Handling objections is a critical part of making sure you can bring your potential client from browser to buyer. The same goes for children.

Objections are the reasons your client doesn't want to buy or your child doesn't want to do what you are asking them to do. The best way to handle objections is to anticipate them first.

We will pretend it is your job to sell whatzits. Why would a customer decide *not* to buy a whatzit? Are they expensive? Are they a luxury? Do all their neighbors have a whatzit? Is a whatzit a quality product? Do they *want* a whatzit? Do they *need* a whatzit?

We will pretend that our customer might object to the expense and quality of the whatzit. By anticipating these concerns, we can think of ways to handle the objections. Perhaps we have a no-interest payment plan. Maybe we have a video to show them that details the quality control process.

The same goes for kiddos. Let's take an easy example. You need your kid to take a bath. Of course, he doesn't want to take a bath. You could fight and yell. You could turn it into a battle of wills. You could endure screaming and crying—both his and yours. You could end the night exhausted and defeated, albeit with a clean kid.

Or…you could listen and handle his objections.

He hates a bath because he hates putting his face underwater. You could use the faucet to shampoo his head instead. He hates a bath because he has to stop playing with his monster trucks. You could choose bath-time monster trucks that only get to be used in the bath. He hates a bath because it takes too long. You could set a timer and make it a race, a game.

None of these small changes make bath time any harder for you. Nothing makes it take longer or become more of a hassle. It is all about the messaging.

FOCUS ON THE BENEFITS

You have to make your kids or your clients want what you have to offer. You have to make them desire it. You have to show them what is in it for them.

Focusing on the benefits is not a focus on what you think is a benefit or on the features of what you are trying to sell. Kids don't care that their shots will keep them healthy. This is a benefit for you, not for them. Clients don't care that your patented process has eighteen iron-clad com-

PEOPLE DON'T JUST WANT SOMETHING AWESOME. THEY WANT SOMETHING AWESOME FOR THEM.

ponents versus twenty. They want to know how it will make their life better, their company better, or their world better.

People don't just want something awesome. They want something awesome for *them*.

We used to go to the Farmer's Market every Sunday. My kids didn't care that we were getting fresh vegetables to keep them healthy. They didn't care that our meat was grass-fed or that our eggs were pastured. They cared that halfway through our walk there was a fresh-made beignet stand—a deep-fried French pastry covered in powdered sugar. They cared that, at the end, after passing stand after stand, there was a playground with two-story slides.

So, we didn't say, "Who wants to go to the Farmer's Market?!" We said, "Who wants beignets?!"

BE PERSUASIVE

Ahhh…the art of persuasion. Some people seem to be born persuaders. Charming in every way, some people just seem to compel people to follow them.

Not all of us are so lucky.

Fortunately, there are simple techniques to help you be more persuasive that can function at work and at home.

APPEAL TO AUTHORITY

Appealing to authority is pointing to research or a prominent person to justify your idea or convince someone to believe your argument. When you use this method, be sure that you are pointing to someone that is *actually* respected by the person you are hoping to persuade. The principal of the school might be a great for your Honor Roll student, not so much for the one who spends a lot of time in detention.

Work: A recent study found that we learn better when we see, hear, and act on the training material. I think we should revise our training plans for next week's conference.

Home: "Insert name of favorite YouTube celebrity" said that she never drinks diet soda. I don't think you should either.

APPEAL TO REASON

Presenting facts, logic, numbers, and other rational information is a way of appealing to reason. Although this strategy can work for older children, it usually isn't very useful for the little ones. Toddlers and preschoolers are not notoriously reasonable.

Work: Just look at the data. Every year, this investment is turning a profit, even when similar stocks are experiencing market declines.

Home: When you go for a run on Saturday mornings, your stats are always better in your baseball game. Maybe you should think about adding a run to your pregame plan?

APPEAL TO EMOTION

Appealing to emotion can feel…sleazy. The goal here is not to manipulate but instead to show the person why they will feel a certain way in a certain situation. It doesn't have to be deceitful.

Work: Think about how good you will feel when this project is submitted! Let's stay late and get it done!

Home: I know you will make the right decision because you love your brother very much. (Often used at our house when attempting to extract an undesired apology.)

APPEAL TO TRUST

If you are honest and truthful, people will trust you. At work, it can take time to build relationships of trust. At home, if you are consistent and honest, your kids will trust you, too.

Work: I really think you are making the right move in accepting the promotion.

Home: Trust me, you don't want to see what happens if you leave food in your room for too many days!

APPEAL TO BELONGING

Belonging is the feeling of being part of a group, community, or society. It is feeling like you are on the inside instead of the outside. It is the reason that the door-to-door salesman selling solar panels tells you that your two neighbors just signed up too. Be careful here. While you may want your child to succumb to positive peer pressure, like everyone turning in their homework on time, you don't want them following just any peer pressure, like skipping school.

Work: The team voted, and we unanimously think a new social media plan is necessary to get big results.

Home: Emma's mom just texted me, and she is dressing up for the dance. Are you sure you don't want to put on your costume?

REPEAT, REPEAT, REPEAT

If at first you don't succeed, try and try again. Repeat your message to ensure it is heard and understood.

Work: Our full strategy for getting this project off the ground is prepared to beat the original timeline, prepared to beat the original budget, and prepared to beat the competitors to market.

Home: (*singing while house cleaning*) Teamwork makes the dream work! Teamwork makes the dream work! Teamwork makes the dream work!

BE HONEST

No one will ever listen to you, will ever respect you, or will ever follow your lead if you are not diligently honest. The supermom secret of marketing is never about lying, not to your co-workers and certainly not to your family.

Enough said.

SUPERMOM SHORTCUT • THE SECRET OF MARKETING • CHAPTER WRAP UP

WHAT WE LEARNED

Supermoms know how to present things to their colleagues, clients, and children to make them want to listen. They know how to make people feel important and handle any objections that come their way. They know how to use marketing strategies typically used in the workplace to ensure the right message is heard at work and home.

HOW WE APPLY IT

We reviewed a number of standard "marketing techniques" that can help us to better communicate with the people in our world:

- Listen and Learn
- Tell a Good Story
- Handle Objections
- Focus on Benefits
- Be Persuasive
- Be Honest

ONE SMALL STEP

Stop lying. Right now. You need to be honest at work and at home if you want to be successful *and* happy. There is no joy in dishonesty.

WHAT COMES NEXT

Where do we go from here? How can we continue to thrive as career-driven, successful, and powerful moms?

CONCLUSION
WHERE DO WE GO FROM HERE?

THESE SECRETS AREN'T FOR KEEPING

"Some days you might wish you weren't juggling work life and home life. You may even let your mind wander to what the grass is like on the other side… But then you look down at your feet and realize they're planted in some pretty lush greens. The blades might be a bit wild and unruly, but boy are they rich and vibrant. So you keep walking in your beautifully untamed meadow, one day at a time."

— Ashley Johnson, *The Grit and Grace Project*[57]

Supermoms are a powerful breed. They develop qualities they never dreamed and skills they never imagined. They do things they never thought possible.

Supermoms have learned the secrets of maintaining a happy team, a happy home, and a happy life. They apply them daily and diligently. They accomplish more in less time, with less effort.

Supermoms have learned to avoid burnout, limit overwhelm, and know that balance is a lie.

Supermoms have it all. They *happily* have it all.

The secrets in this book are not hard. They do require work, but anyone with the grit and determination can apply them to be successful. You can be a happy, career-driven, amazing mom. You can have the job, the home, and the family of your dreams. You do not have to sacrifice one for another. You just have to want it and be willing to work for it.

These secrets aren't for keeping. Do you know a mom that is struggling? Share a chapter. Share a quick tip. Share the book.

We can help each other get everything we want and nothing we don't. We can have it all, if we want it.

SUPERMOMS HAVE IT ALL. THEY HAPPILY HAVE IT ALL.

CAN YOU HELP?

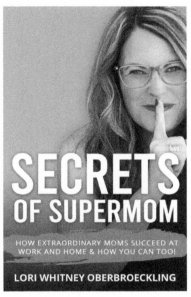

Thank You For Reading My Book!
I always appreciate your feedback, and I love hearing what
readers have to say.
I need your input to make my future books better.
Please leave me an honest review on Amazon letting me
know what you thought of the book.
Thanks so much!

Rooting for you,
Lori Whitney Oberbroeckling

ABOUT THE AUTHOR

Lori Whitney Oberbroeckling is a certified supermom. She is a wife and mom to four tiny humans, all while working in corporate America and nurturing several side-hustles. She helps moms who want it all develop the skills, habits, and confidence to happily have it all. She has a bachelor's degree in psychology with graduate training in marriage and family therapy, and a history in teaching and counseling. She lives with her family in Phoenix, Arizona.

You can connect with Lori at www.secretsofsupermom.com.
Facebook: @secretsofsupermom
Instagram: @secretsofsupermom

ENDNOTES & RECOMMENDATIONS FOR FURTHER READING

CHAPTER 1

1   Clear, J. (2018). Atomic Habits: An Easy & Proven Way to Build Good Habits & Break Bad Ones (Illustrated ed.). Avery.

2   Duhigg, C. (2014). The Power of Habit: Why We Do What We Do in Life and Business. Random House Trade Paperbacks

3   Burchard, B. (2017). High Performance Habits: How Extraordinary People Become That Way (Later Printing ed.). Hay House Inc.

4   Duhigg, C. (2014). The Power of Habit: Why We Do What We Do in Life and Business. Random House Trade Paperbacks

5   Clear, J. (2018). Atomic Habits: An Easy & Proven Way to Build Good Habits & Break Bad Ones (Illustrated ed.). Avery.

6   Fogg, B.J.,Ph.D (2019). Tiny Habits: The Small Changes That Change Everything (Illustrated ed.). Houghton Mifflin Harcourt.

CHAPTER 2

7   Winfrey, O. (2004, May). Body Confidence. O, The Oprah Magazine. https://libquotes.com/oprah-winfrey/quote/lbe3m7r

8   Williamson, M. (1996). A Return to Love: Reflections on the Principles of "A Course in Miracles" (Reissue ed.). HarperOne.

9   Oxford University Press (OUP). (2020). Confidence. Lexico.Com. https://www.lexico.com/en/definition/confidence

10   Confidence | Oxford Advanced American Dictionary at OxfordLearnersDictionaries.com. (2020). Https://Www.Oxfordlearnersdictionaries.Com/Us/Definition/American_english/Confidence. https://www.oxfordlearnersdictionaries.com/us/definition/american_english/confidence

11   Dweck, C. S. (2007). Mindset: The New Psychology of Success (Illustrated ed.). Ballantine Books.

CHAPTER 3

12   Elrod, H. (2012). The Miracle Morning: The Not-So-Obvious Secret Guaranteed to Transform Your Life (Before 8AM) (1st Paperback Edition). Hal Elrod.

13   Popular Quotes. (2020). Https://Www.Goodreads.Com/Quotes/. https://www.goodreads.com/quotes/

14   Ferriss, T. (2007). The 4-Hour Workweek: Escape 9-5, Live Anywhere, and Join the New Rich. Crown.

15   Keller, G., & Papasan, J. (2013). The ONE Thing: The Surprisingly Simple Truth Behind Extraordinary Results (Illustrated ed.). Bard Press

16   Ackerman, C. (2020, September 1). What is Gratitude and Why is It So Important? [2019 Update]. PositivePsychology.Com. https://positivepsychology.com/gratitude-appreciation/

CHAPTER 4

17   A quote by John C. Maxwell. (2020). Goodreads.Com. https://www.goodreads.com/quotes/3216300-if-you-want-to-do-a-few-small-things-right

18   Self Motivation. (2020, February 27). Ask for help and don't stop until you get it | Motivational story [Video]. YouTube. https://www.youtube.com/watch?v=hafAYE2jp6o&feature=youtu.be

CHAPTER 5

19   Urban, H. M., & Hartwig, D. (2015). The Whole30: The 30-Day Guide to Total Health and Food Freedom (1st Edition). Houghton Mifflin Harcourt.

Recommended reading:

The Whole 30 by Melissa & Dallas Urban

Body Love by Kelly Leveque

The Sugar Impact Diet by JJ. Virgin

The Bulletproof Diet by Dave Asprey

CHAPTER 6

20   Seuss. (1957). The Cat in the Hat (1st ed.). Random House Books for Young Readers.

21   Bennett, R. T. (2020). The Light in the Heart: Inspirational Thoughts for Living Your Best Life. Roy Bennett.

22   Positive attitude toward math predicts math achievement in kids. (2018). News Center. https://med.stanford.edu/news/all-news/2018/01/positive-attitude-toward-math-predicts-math-achievement-in-kids.html

23   How Can Positive Thinking Benefit Your Mind and Body? (2020). Verywell Mind. https://www.verywellmind.com/benefits-of-positive-thinking-2794767

24   Weinstein, N. D. (1980). Unrealistic optimism about future life events. Journal of Personality and Social Psychology, 39(5), 806–820. https://doi.org/10.1037/0022-3514.39.5.806

CHAPTER 7

25   Horowitz, B. (2014). The Hard Thing About Hard Things: Building a Business When There Are No Easy Answers. Harper Business.

26   Gaetani, G. (2015). The noble art of misquoting Camus -- from its origins to the Internet era. Https://Www.Academia.Edu/19617157/The_noble_art_of_misquoting_Camus_from_its_origins_to_the_Internet_era.https://www.academia.edu/19617157/The_noble_art_of_misquoting_Camus_from_its_origins_to_the_Internet_era

27   Covey, S. (1994). The 7 Habits of Highly Effective People: Powerful Lessons in Personal Change (5287th ed.). DC Books.

CHAPTER 8

28   Branson, R. (2016, August 4). My Metric for Success? Happiness. Www.Linkedin.Com. https://www.linkedin.com/pulse/my-metric-success-happiness-richard-branson?trk=mp-reader-card

29   Bennett, R. T. (2020). The Light in the Heart: Inspirational Thoughts for Living Your Best Life. Roy Bennett.

30   Rubin, G. (2012). The Happiness Project (Twenty-fifth Printing ed.). HarperCollins Publishers.

31   Cirino, E. (2018, April 11). What Are the Benefits of Hugging? Healthline. https://www.healthline.com/health/hugging-benefits#2.-Hugs-may-protect-you-against-illness

CHAPTER 9

32   Burchard, B. (2020, August 12). How to Master Motivation. Brendon Burchard. https://brendon.com/blog/how-to-mastermotivation/#:%7E:text=Many%20people%2C%20they've%20gone,emotional%20pull%20towards%20something%20better.&text=When%20we%20lack%20motivation%2C%20it%20is%20a%20slippery%20slope%20to%20suffering.

33   Rubin, G. (2015). Better Than Before: What I Learned About Making and Breaking Habits--to Sleep More, Quit Sugar, Procrastinate Less, and Generally Build a Happier Life (Illustrated ed.). Broadway Books..

34   Clear, J. (2018). Atomic Habits: An Easy & Proven Way to Build Good Habits & Break Bad Ones (Illustrated ed.). Avery.

35   Maslach, C., & Leiter, M. P. (2016). Understanding the burnout experience: recent research and its implications for psychiatry. World Psychiatry: official journal of the World Psychiatric Association (WPA), 15(2), 103–111. https://doi.org/10.1002/wps.20311

36   Gaither, C. (2014, July 13). The Opposite of Burnout – ENGAGEMENT. Http://Www.Clarkgaither.Com/. http://www.clarkgaither.com/the-opposite-of-burnout-engagement/

CHAPTER 10

37   Keen, S. (1992). Fire in the Belly: On Being a Man. Bantam.

38   Angelou, M. (1994). Wouldn't Take Nothing for My Journey Now (Reissue ed.). Bantam.

39   M. (2019, October). Burnout Prevention and Treatment - Help-Guide.org. Https://Www.Helpguide.Org/Articles/Stress/Burnout-Prevention-and-Recovery.Htm#:~:Text=Burnout%20is%20a%20state%20 of,Unable%20to%20meet%20constant%20demands.

40   Covey, S. (1994). The 7 Habits of Highly Effective People: Powerful Lessons in Personal Change (5287th ed.). DC Books.

41   Midland, N. (2020, July). Why Does Stretching Feel Good? A Health Beneficial Pick-Me-Up We All Need. Better Me. https://betterme. world/articles/why-does-stretching-feel-good/

CHAPTER 11

42   Dweck, C. S. (2007). Mindset: The New Psychology of Success (Illustrated ed.). Ballantine Books

43   Dweck, C. S. (2007). Mindset: The New Psychology of Success (Illustrated ed.). Ballantine Books.

44   "shame v. guilt | Brené Brown." 14 Jan. 2013, https://brenebrown. com/blog/2013/01/14/shame-v-guilt/. Accessed 13 Oct. 2020.

CHAPTER 12

45   Tracy, B. (2018, March 7). How to Set Priorities Using the ABCDE Method | Brian Tracy. Brian Tracy's Self Improvement & Professional Development Blog. https://www.briantracy.com/blog/time-management/the-abcde-list-technique-for-setting-priorities/

CHAPTER 13

46   Sivers, D. (2019, October 1). Where to find the hours to make it happen | Derek Sivers. Https://Sive.Rs/Uncomf. https://sive.rs/uncomf

47 Sam Huff. (n.d.). AZQuotes.com. Retrieved September 02, 2020, from AZQuotes.com Web site: https://www.azquotes.com/author/25623-Sam_Huff

48 Parkinson, N. C. (1962). PARKINSON'S LAW: OR THE PURSUIT OF PROGRESS. John Murray.

CHAPTER 14

49 Ferriss, T. (2007). The 4-Hour Workweek: Escape 9-5, Live Anywhere, and Join the New Rich. Crown

50 Paul J. Meyer Quotes (Author of Become the Coach You Were Meant to Be). (2020). Https://Www.Goodreads.Com/. https://www.goodreads.com/author/quotes/135147

51 How to Achieve an Action Mindset (and Stay Disciplined!). (2020, September 3). [Video]. Brendon Burchard. https://brendon.com/blog/achieving-action-mindset/

CHAPTER 15

52 Angelou, M. (1994). Wouldn't Take Nothing for My Journey Now (Reissue ed.). Bantam.

53 Pausch, R., & Zaslow, J. (2008). The Last Lecture (1st ed.). Hyperion.

54 Bradberry, Travis. "How Complaining Rewires Your Brain for Negativity." Entrepreneur, 9 Sept. 2016, http://www.entrepreneur.com

55 Priest, S., & Gass, M. (1997). An Examination of "Problem-Solving" versus "Solution-Focused" Facilitation Styles in a Corporate Setting. Journal of Experiential Education, 20(1), 34–39. https://doi.org/10.1177/10538259970two-hundred0106

CHAPTER 16

56   Miller, D. (2017). Building a StoryBrand: Clarify Your Message So Customers Will Listen (Illustrated ed.). HarperCollins Leadership

CONCLUSION

57   Johnson, A. (2020). 5 Quotes That Will Encourage You, Working (Super) Mom. Https://Thegritandgraceproject.Org/. https://thegritand-graceproject.org/life-and-culture/5-quotes-that-will-encourage-you-working-super-mom